THE WASHINGTON PAPERS
Volume VI

53: East-West Trade: Problems, Prospects, Issues

Alec Nove

THE CENTER FOR STRATEGIC AND INTERNATIONAL STUDIES
Georgetown University, Washington, D.C.

SAGE PUBLICATIONS
Beverly Hills / London

Printed in the United States of America

For information address:

SAGE Publications, Inc.
275 South Beverly Drive
Beverly Hills, California 90212

SAGE Publications Ltd
28 Banner Street
London EC1Y 8QE

International Standard Book Number 0-8039-1039-8

Library of Congress Catalog Card No. 78-52025

FIRST PRINTING

When citing a Washington Paper, please use the proper form. Remember to cite the series title and include the paper number. One of the two following formats can be adapted (depending on the style manual used):

(1) HASSNER, P. (1973) "Europe in the Age of Negotiation." The Washington Papers, I, 8. Beverly Hills and London: Sage Pubns.

OR

(2) Hassner, Pierre. 1973. *Europe in the Age of Negotiation.* The Washington Papers, vol. 1, no. 8. Beverly Hills and London: Sage Publications.

CONTENTS

I. INTRODUCTION

This paper will examine the following questions. What is the importance of East-West trade to the East and to the West? What is its historical background? What is the relationship between trade and détente? Does the Soviet bloc gain more from trade than we do? What about the mounting volume of credits and of Eastern indebtedness? Is all this in the West's interest? What has been, is, and will be the role of Comecon (CMEA) under Soviet leadership? What policy options are open to the West in general, the United States in particular? Is greater interdependence a desirable state of affairs? What leverage, what chance of influencing Soviet political and military postures, does their growing dependence on Western technology and grain give us, and in what situations is it appropriate to use such weapons?

A few words of explanation and definition. "East" will, for the present purpose, mean the Soviet Union and its European allies. No attempt will be made here to analyze trade with non-European members of Comecon, that is to say Mongolia, Cuba, or China. U.S. trade policies toward China and Cuba have a very different history and raise very different issues. China, the world's most populous nation, will doubtless play a growing role in international commerce, but information is scarce and in any case I openly recognize my incompetence to write anything worth reading about China. The "West" here means the industrialized "capitalist" world, and includes Japan.

I do not intend to inflict a mass of statistics upon the reader, but of course there must be some. Part of the figures will be in dollars and taken from UN publications or from the trade statistics of the West. Others will be in the currencies of the Eastern countries or converted from these currencies into dollars. But these currencies have their peculiarities. In the first place, for reasons to be explained, domestic currency and prices have very little indeed to do with the prices used in foreign trade. Thus if we know that Soviet or Polish output is worth 100 million rubles or zloty in their internal prices, it tells us very little about the dollar value of the goods, or what they would bring if exported. If, however, foreign trade statistics record the export of goods worth 100 million rubles (or zloty), then this is foreign-trade currency, which it is usually possible to convert at the official rate of exchange, because goods in foreign trade are valued (more or less) at capitalist world prices. Therefore we can take 100 million rubles in 1970 (say) as equal to 133 million dollars. The words "more or less" are not just scholastic qualification: sometimes trade takes place at prices which, for various reasons, are above or below world prices. To take oil as an example, in 1970 the Soviet Union sold oil to its Comecon partners at prices above those it charged to Western Europe, while in 1974 the Comecon partners benefited from pre-Yom Kippur War prices (which have been raised since). All statistics, including the UN-published ones in dollars, are affected by such problems of valuation and conversion.

What, then, is a ruble "worth"? A whole article could be devoted to this topic. Briefly, the answer depends on who holds the ruble and what the holder is allowed to buy. Rubles are not convertible, i.e., they cannot legally be exchanged into any other currency except with specific authorization. For some purposes they have no value: thus any tourist knows that in the *Beryozka* shops in Russia nothing can be bought with rubles (or other Eastern currencies); one must pay in convertible Western currency. A Soviet manager with a ruble bank balance may only spend it (e.g., for purchase of materials, even Soviet materials) if he holds a planners' allocation certificate. A Soviet citizen can buy, for rubles at internal retail prices, whatever might be in the shops. Some items are by our standards cheap, others dear, still others unobtainable at any price. A Comecon trading partner would be unable to purchase freely in the Soviet Union: rubles earned in trade are used in what amount to barter deals, annual quotas which are the subject of bilateral bargaining. True, there is now the so-called "transferable ruble," but, as we shall see, its use is still very limited. Finally there is the black market or free rate, for which rubles can be obtained in Zurich or from touts (strictly illegal) in Russia. This is several times higher than the official rate, and higher also than any conceivable purchasing-power parity: it reflects the fact that ordinary Soviet citizens are unable to obtain dollars legally, and also that some goods cannot be obtained for rubles at all. So the "worth" of a ruble is not at all easy to determine, may even in the circumstances be indeterminable.

II. AN HISTORICAL VIEW OF EAST-WEST TRADE

The Foreign Trade Monopoly

One of the earliest acts of the Soviet government was to decree the state monopoly of foreign trade. The same was done by other Communist governments once in power. Originally this meant that private individuals or private firms were prevented from buying and selling across state borders. It has come to mean that all foreign deals are conducted under the Ministry of Foreign Trade, through one of its many specialized corporations (such as *Stankoimport,* for machinery, *Exportles* for timber; some, despite their designations, deal with both import and export business). The ministry guards this monopoly jealously against attempts by other state enterprises to be allowed to import and export. In some Eastern countries, for instance Hungary, a number of state enterprises *are* allowed to enter foreign trade directly. In the Soviet Union, however, this is still exceptional, consisting almost entirely of border trade (e.g., Leningrad-Finland, Far East-Japan), and even this to a strictly limited extent.

It is sometimes said that this gives a commercial advantage to the Soviet Union: their corporations are each monopolists in their field, and they can play Western traders off against each other. Certainly Soviet textbooks do assert that it would be quite wrong to allow Soviet enterprises to compete against one another. However, any advantages are, in the opinion of many, counterbalanced by serious disadvantages. In the first place, there is little sign that the member states of Comecon coordinate their deals with the West, or that they bargain as one unit. Second, and much more important, the specialized foreign trade corporations act as a barrier between the Soviet producer or customer and the foreign market, with consequences that have been the subject of many complaints. True, in some spheres the specialized corporations are unchallengeable experts: for instance, Russians have been trading in timber and grain for centuries—but this is not typical. Requests for imported products or market information become enmeshed in a bureaucratic structure. The ministry's sub-units are compulsory intermediates which can be clumsy and cause frustrating delays. Imagine a situation in which an American business has to deal through one official trading agency, and is allowed neither to operate directly nor to change to another agency if dissatisfied with the service provided. This would hardly seem to be a recipe for efficiency.

The Place of Foreign Trade in Soviet Planning

The *size* of foreign trade in relation to national production will not be our concern in this section. My purpose here is to sketch in how a country such as the Soviet Union "fits" trade into its planning system. (Some of her East European allies have modified the system so it is no longer of universal application.)

The first and most fundamental point is that resources are allocated by the central planners, under the authority of the Communist Party leadership, which acts as the supreme board of directors of USSR Inc., the largest corporation in the world. They decide not only broad economic strategy and priorities, but also, in the last resort, what investments should be made, what each productive unit should be producing, how much should be paid in wages, the prices at which all these transactions should take place, and a whole variety of detail down to and including the "tying" by the plan of customer-enterprise to supplier-enterprise. Managers are, as a rule, not free to sell to whom they please, or to buy their inputs from the partner they choose. Of course, the details are not, save in super-priority areas (like ICBMs), the direct concern of the *top* leadership: such tasks are delegated to industrial ministries, industrial associations, supply agencies, and so on. In practice, as may be imagined, proposals put up from subordinates affect the orders they receive, but plan-orders are the basis of the activities of managers.

The system suffers from bureaucratic deformations, which will not be our concern here (we have problems too!), except perhaps to mention two areas in which it is rather conspicuously unsuccessful. One is agriculture, the other is the diffusion of technical progress. The reasons are in fact fundamentally identical: in both these areas a key role is played by initiative from those directly involved in production, while remote central control is frustrating and ineffective because precisely what needs doing is usually not known at the center. Central planning has some advantages too, which show up well, for instance, in the planning of electricity supply, oil developments in Siberia, and the production of nuclear submarines. It is *not* my intention to write off the whole Soviet economy as hopelessly inefficient. (This point will be of considerable importance later on, as we shall see.)

Where does foreign trade come in? It is the task of the planners to make available for export the amount required to enable imports to be paid for (taking into account also gold sales, use of reserves, and borrowing). In the short run this can call for decisions involving limits on allocations for domestic customers and/or Comecon allies, as is happening now in the case of oil. In the longer run, of course, investments can be made to enlarge output of the exporting branches. The leadership indicates priorities for imports, and at the same time requests for imports are made from below, from enterprise management, from the internal trade organs, and so on. Out of all this emerges an import and export plan. It is then the task of the foreign trade organs to sell at the best price they can, to buy as cheaply as they are able. Their actions are insulated from internal prices, which simply do not concern them: if, converted at the official exchange rate, the result is a loss, there will be a budgetary subsidy; if a profit, it will go to the state budget.

The above is, inevitably, much too simple a picture. Soviet

trade planners are not in fact free to sell or to buy on the basis of purely economic criteria. The Soviet Union has a large number of bilateral agreements, e.g., within Comecon and with many developing countries. Trade agreements concluded with Western countries may also commit the Soviet Union to buy specified quantities of certain items as a precondition for obtaining access to the Western market in question. Some currencies are convertible, others are not. So in practice the trade plan has to be broken up into subplans for exchanges with specific countries or groups of countries, and this modifies the priorities of the planners and the behavior of the trade corporations. For example, wine may not be high on the list of import needs, but Algeria needs to sell wine to pay for Soviet deliveries. Pepsi-Cola may not be top priority in know-how imports, but the deal helps to sell Soviet vodka in the United States. Some natural gas and oil are committed by long-term agreements to particular countries. Supplies of convertible currency free of any strings or commitments are limited. So there are many complex trade-offs, bargains to be made in the everyday business of Soviet trade. Politics, too, plays a role. For instance, if Algeria were unfriendly, goods saleable elsewhere would not be exchanged for wine. If President Carter is hostile, fewer orders may be placed in America. But we will be discussing the *politics* of Soviet trade at length elsewhere in this paper.

Priorities can and do alter. Heavy machinery and modern technology remain high on the list, but an increasing share of Soviet imports, even from capitalist countries, consists of goods used directly or indirectly for the consumption of citizens: grain, of course, but also some consumer goods and the know-how and equipment to make them (the Fiat car plant is one example), as well as meat, coffee, bananas, etc. Other Eastern countries also have to pay attention to the citizens' needs, if only to avoid dangerous discontent. These smaller countries, for obvious reasons, rely a great deal more on foreign trade. The Soviet Union contains within its borders a high proportion of its needs for raw materials and fuels, which is certainly not the case of Hungary, Poland, or Czechoslovakia, for instance.

Given the nature of the system, one can see the logic of centralizing foreign trade in a specialized ministry, which is closely linked in its operations to the central planning organs. As already indicated, these planning organs decide not only economic and political priorities, they are also supreme managers and resource-allocators. Therefore, export orders are incorporated in the plans of the producing enterprises, the plan also providing for the delivery to these enterprises of the necessary machines, fuel, materials, components, freight cars, etc. Similarly, the supply plans of the various users of imported goods (factories, internal trade organs, transport undertakings, etc.) incorporate these goods. All this has, further, to be coordinated with the plans for payments in foreign currencies, modified where necessary as a result of trade negotiations or unexpected export opportunities or import needs (e.g., if the harvest is bad), and so on. One can readily see, within such a system, why the planners resist the proposal that managers of enterprises be allowed to engage in foreign transactions: after all, they are not allowed to buy and sell freely within the Soviet Union itself!

Perhaps the best parallel would be to imagine an American supermarket chain with centralized procurement and stock control: one would not then expect the manager of the supermarkets located in Kansas City to be allowed to buy goods from Japan or Czechoslovakia, nor would the headquarters staff welcome a proposal that he (or she) should have such powers.

I must again mention the fact that certain Eastern countries have relaxed the degree of central control over foreign trade, in connection with reforms that have freed management from total subordination to central production and supply plans.

Of course, even in the Soviet Union some flexibility has been introduced by sheer necessity. The center cannot possibly control everything, and initiatives from management make a considerable difference in what actually happens. Experts from industrial ministries can be brought into negotiations on specific trade deals that concern them. Nor should one exaggerate the degree of coherence of the political-economic system. The different ministries, republics, and departments are in a real sense *administrative competitors* for resources, including those entering into foreign trade. There is a kind of "centralized pluralism." But the conflict between interest groups is contained within the party-government structure; conflicts are, in the last analysis, reconciled within the Politbureau of the ruling party. So far the basic principles of planning have resisted efforts to change them, and so the foreign trade sector remains firmly in the place to which it logically "belongs" within the centralized structure of management and control.

Early History

East-West trade was, of course, synonymous with Soviet trade with the capitalist world, until after the events of World War II brought other socialist countries into being. When Soviet Russia emerged from the ruin and chaos of the civil war, it was clear to Lenin and his comrades that foreign trade had to play a big role in reconstruction and in industrial development. Russia before the revolution was already in the throes of rapid industrialization, and so the first actions of the regime were to reconstruct wartime damage and encourage the restoration of agriculture, relying at first on the private peasantry and allowing some small-scale private enterprise in towns also, though foreign trade was a state monopoly. It would obviously be necessary to import a wide range of machinery and to seek the help of Western experts. Russia was traditionally an exporter of grain, timber, furs, minerals, and also oil (in 1900 Russia was, for a short period, the world's biggest oil producer). It was Lenin's view that the capitalist world needed Russia's materials badly, and also needed Russia as a market. Thus, once the civil war was over, he was all for using this "economic weapon" to secure political recognition as well as economic advantages. The immediate difficulty was to find enough to export, especially as the peasants sold less grain (they and their animals consumed more of it than before the revolution). But trade increased (from the abysmal levels of 1921) as the following figures show:

(Millions of Rubles)

	1920	1921-1922	1922-1923	1923-1924	1924-1925	1925-1926	1926-1927
Exports	1.1	49.8	105.0	292.6	453.0	551.5	632.7
Imports	22.5	212.6	116.5	183.1	567.3	593.1	559.5

Source: *Vneshnaya torgovlya SSR, 1918-66.* The rubles were converted into present-value rubles by source. Statistics at this period were for the agricultural year July-June.

The situation was transformed by three circumstances: the launching of the first of many industrializing five-year plans, the Great Depression, and the increased fear of war. Together they help to explain the precipitous decline of Soviet trade after 1931:

	1929	1930	1931	1932	1933	1938
Exports	724.3	812.7	636.1	450.8	388.7	229.8
Imports	690.5	830.3	866.5	552.5	273.1	245.3

(*Source:* as above)

Imported machinery and equipment, expressed as a percentage of productive installations, fell from 19 percent in 1930 to 2.4 percent in 1933 (Ekonomicheskie svyazi vostok-zapad, 1976: 24).

The first five-year plan (1928-1932) required very large increases in imports of machinery from the West, as it set extremely ambitious targets of industrial growth. At the same time, the Western depression led to a very rapid fall in prices of raw materials, greatly worsening the balance-of-payments situation. The need to pay for machinery led to draconian measures. The fall in agricultural production, due to the collectivization of agriculture, which most peasants hated, compelled the government to use the harshest measures to obtain grain for export, causing starvation in some areas. There was compulsory collection of gold from the people, even the sale of some old masters from the Hermitage museum. Imports of so-called nonessentials were heavily cut, gravely affecting the consumer goods industries (thus wool textile production fell sharply, because imports of wool were greatly reduced). On the positive side, the Great Depression encouraged Western firms to accept Soviet orders and grant credits, and unemployed industrial experts were easy to recruit. The third of the factors mentioned above, fear of war, had the effect of enhancing the priority of heavy industry (which is the basis of arms-making capacity) and also the emphasis on self-sufficiency. No doubt Stalin recalled that the Russian army in World War I had greatly suffered from the fact that machinery and engineering relied so much on imports, which were cut off by wartime blockade. Therefore, and particularly after Hitler had come to power, every effort was made to make Russian heavy industry independent of imports. Hence the tendency to autarky, which some have regarded as an essential feature of the system, but which was to some extent forced.

Wartime industrial aid, through lend-lease, played a significant role, especially in those sectors where Soviet industry had remained underdeveloped (e.g., motor transport, radio equipment, etc.), and to make up for productive capacity lost in the retreat. However, it is only right to stress the immense, indeed astonishing, achievements of Soviet war industry from 1941 to 1945.

With the war's end, there was again ruin, hunger, and reconstruction, accompanied by great difficulties in finding the means of payment for needed imports. Further, the recovery of Soviet trade with the West was soon checked by the rising tide of political friction, culminating in the Western embargoes of the Korean War period.

The Second World War brought into being communist-led regimes in Eastern Europe (and in 1949 in China also). Following the rejection (on Soviet orders) of Marshall aid, these countries found themselves under multiple pressures. By tradition their economic links were with the West: the trade between these countries and the Soviet Union had been very small before the war. Some of these countries (the future East Germany, Hungary, Romania) had to bear the burden of reparation for having fought against the Soviet Union, which exerted pressure on them all to trade with it by preference, on terms decided by Moscow. Indeed, two ministers of foreign trade, in Czechoslovakia and in Bulgaria, were executed by hanging for the crime of bargaining too hard with the Soviet Union. At the same time, Western embargoes were disrupting their trade links with the West, compelling them willy-nilly to rely more on their Soviet senior partners. East-West trade languished, a victim of politics.

In 1949 came the foundation of Comecon or CMEA (the Council for Mutual Economic Assistance) but in the first period of its existence this body played a minor role. The Soviet Union controlled its satellites directly, and was concerned to prevent their independent collaboration (a consequence of fears generated by the defection of Yugoslavia). Thus one Hungarian official told me that a proposal he had made in 1949 for an agreement

TABLE 1
Trade with the Industrialized West ($ million)

	1960	1965	1970
Bulgaria			
Exports	67.7	155.0	255.8
Imports	83.8	237.4	321.0
Czechoslovakia			
Exports	304.2	439.2	746.4
Imports	325.6	486.7	879.9
East Germany			
Exports	441.2	630.6	1,057.5
Imports	511.0	637.9	1,350.5
Hungary			
Exports	182.9	321.5	626.0
Imports	234.3	379.9	699.1
Poland			
Exports	369.7	600.8	933.0
Imports	483.1	597.9	970.0
Romania			
Exports	145.5	254.2	547.3
Imports	147.5	347.2	753.2
Soviet Union (with Rubles)			
Exports	913.3	1,346.1	2,153.9
Imports	1,004.0	1,469.5	2,540.1

Sources (1960-1970): "Reorientation and commercial relations of the economies of Eastern Europe" (Joint Economic Committee of U.S. Congress 1974), and UN (E.C.E.) Economic Surveys of Europe.

with Poland, under which Hungary, which lacks good coal, would get its coal from Poland, was vetoed because of Moscow's opposition to such deals.

Then Stalin died, and a wind of change blew. Among the many things that changed were the following that affected foreign trade:

(a) A thaw in the cold war; a shift in Soviet emphasis toward "peaceful coexistence"; and a relaxation in Western embargoes (except, at first, by the United States).

(b) A greater willingness in the Soviet Union to recognize her relative technological backwardness, the advantages of trade with the West, and the disadvantages of isolation.

(c) A greater degree of autonomy for smaller Eastern countries. No more ministers would be hanged for bargaining too hard with the Soviet Union. The countries concerned became able to take much more initiative in developing their own trade links with the West. The key date here is 1956, the year of destalinization and the Polish and Hungarian events. Henceforth efforts would be made to restore and extend economic links with the West.

(d) At the same time, Comecon began to come alive, with a gradual increase in joint planning and mutual specialization. Trade between Comecon members also began to increase steeply.

(e) A change in internal priorities toward the consumer, affecting the content of plans and also of trade—though priority was still given to heavy industry—and there remained (and remains) an immense pent-up demand for Western goods. When, in 1963, the grain crop was hit by drought, Khrushchev ordered major grain purchases in the West, claiming with some justice that Stalin would not have done it.

The figures in Table 1 show what happened to East-West trade.

Policy and Attitudes to East-West Trade Until 1970

On the Western side, apart from maintaining a joint list of so-called strategic products whose export to the East was banned (the "COCOM" list), there was no effective coordination. West European countries and Japan took commercial opportunities as they offered themselves. The main limit on expansion was Eastern ability to pay and to expand their exports to the West. The United States hung back, taking—especially under John Foster Dulles—a much more negative view of the whole process. Symbolic of U.S. attitudes at this period was the affair of the large-diameter oil pipe. It is worth dwelling on, because it represents a test case for a view still widespread today, which has profound consequences for the future and potential of East-West trade if it seriously affects policy decisions. The date of the occurrence was 1961.

The Soviet planners faced the need to lay more pipelines, to bring oil from eastern areas to the center and west of the country. (This is still an urgent matter for them.) Domestic production capacity for pipe was (and is) insufficient. They therefore sought to place a large order in West Germany. Pipe was not on the COCOM list of "strategic" products. However, it was (correctly) calculated in Washington that denial of pipe would inhibit Soviet economic development in the short run, and create awkward problems. Therefore pressure was exerted on the West German authorities, who in those days felt themselves much more dependent on America than they are today, and the West Germans refused the order. This is past history. The Soviets have been buying pipe from many Western countries, including Germany, for years now. But history may repeat itself. The point is: is it appropriate or desirable for us to study the urgency of Soviet need and deny supplies as and when we think it will cause most embarrassment and damage? If we act thus, or the Soviet planners expect us to act thus, this will greatly affect their willingness to rely on East-West trade and to commit resources for its expansion. We will return later to the question of whether we wish this to happen.

In any case, this negative attitude diminished through the 1960s. The Soviets tried to expand trade, while trying to derive political as well as economic dividends from this. Their vulgar Marxist philosophy inclines them to the belief that businessmen —capitalists—dominate Western policies, so the Soviets assume that if many capitalists find dealings with the East profitable, the aims of Soviet foreign policy will be helped. As for the planners in the smaller countries, they were not unmindful of the advantage of relying less on their powerful Soviet ally, especially as they knew Western goods were usually of superior quality.

To expand trade, however, it was necessary to expand exports to the West; and, as will be shown in greater detail later, it is hard to make available for Western markets goods of the needed quantity and quality. As the figures in Table 1 show, the volume of trade did indeed rise rapidly. But the East made it known that it would place more orders if long-term credits would be extended. Over this question the West, with America in the lead, took a cautiously negative line. Long-term credits to the Soviet Union were actively discouraged at first.

Then, either because of the psychological impact of Brezhnev's détente policy, or through the pressure of businessmen seeking orders, or maybe just attrition through time, the barriers to credit crumbled. A serious Soviet book (Ekonomichestie svyazi vostok-zapad, 1976: 126-127) on problems of East-West trade has interpreted what occurred as follows:

> Under the influence of détente, the credit policy of the West towards socialist countries altered substantially. One of the most characteristic changes was the gradual "depoliticization" of export credits, an ever greater transformation of credits from a political weapon into a normal means of developing mutually beneficial collaboration, an ever greater economic, commercial approach to crediting stable and long-term links between the partners.

Whether or not one accepts this as a correct interpretation, the fact remains that credits and loans became much more freely available by various routes and from various sources, which we will be examining in due course, and this without any specific political decision that can be dated or attributed.

East-West Trade in the 1970s

No apologies are needed for introducing the facts in the form of statistical tables (see Table 2).

It can be seen at once that the *value* of East-West trade has rapidly risen, but part of the increase is due to the sharp upsurge in world prices. The impact of these price rises has been very unequal as between the various Eastern countries, and the balance of trade has been affected in various ways also by internal policies.

Take the Soviet Union first. As the figures show, it had a chronic deficit with the West, which was met in the main by gold sales. (The Soviet Union is the second biggest gold producer after South Africa, and is so sensitive about its gold that it publishes no figures about output or reserves, or, for that matter, about the balance of payments.) The huge increase in prices of fuels

TABLE 2
Western Trade With the East Since 1970 ($ million)

	1970	1971	1972	1973	1974	1975	1976
Bulgaria							
Exports	329	323	348	491	847	1,102	926
Imports	223	230	251	341	383	365	450
Czechoslovakia							
Exports	786	916	1,000	1,352	1,746	1,880	2,064
Imports	675	771	884	1,188	1,431	1,523	1,571
East Germany							
Exports	439	504	636	752	,001	1,130	1,269
Imports	381	396	476	611	885	962	991
Hungary							
Exports	628	743	832	1,112	1,792	1,836	1,818
Imports	497	535	741	1,025	1,251	1,158	1,330
Poland							
Exports	893	1,057	1,679	3,193	4,590	5,498	5,501
Imports	990	1,128	1,409	1,986	2,685	2,956	3,343
Romania							
Exports	706	757	990	1,354	2,054	2,005	2,020
Imports	514	580	737	1,024	1,474	1,552	1,808
Soviet Union							
Exports	2,652	2,652	3,904	5,785	7,523	12,532	13,750
Imports	2,610	2,843	3,199	4,947	7,780	8,201	10,058

Source: OECD, Paris. (NOTE that these figures are from **Western** countries' statistical returns, and therefore do not (and cannot) precisely match figures taken from Eastern trade accounts used by the UN and elsewhere. "West" here includes only Western Europe plus U.S.A., Canada and Japan.)

and materials, oil especially, greatly improved her position during 1973 and especially 1974, during which year the Soviet Union recorded a small trade *surplus* with the West as a whole, a most unusual event.

Faced with an unexpectedly favorable conjuncture, and with greatly increased willingness of Western countries and banks to extend credits, the Soviet Union increased substantially its purchases from the West, of machinery especially, and placed large orders for more. Then in 1975 came a shock: Soviet exports fell, as a result of the Western recession, while imports rose steeply, partly as a result of orders already placed, and partly as a consequence of the deplorable harvest of 1975, which led to very large purchases being made in the United States and Canada. To cap everything, the price of gold fell. Therefore the Soviet Union ran into short-term payments difficulties and its debt increased steeply. Some of this increase was certainly unplanned and unexpected.

As an exporter of raw materials and fuels to her more industrialized partners (East Germany, Czechoslovakia, Poland, Hungary), the Soviet Union stood to gain from the sharp rise in world prices. However, in 1974 she was still, under old agreements, charging Comecon countries pre-1973 prices. For example, in 1974, Soviet oil and oil products were sold at an average of 58.20 rubles per ton to Italy, but at 21.00 to Hungary. However, this could not last, and prices in East-East trade are being moved up by stages to the average level of world prices in the previous five years. The net effect, though with delay, is to improve Soviet terms of trade with other Eastern countries. (Nonetheless, in 1976, Soviet oil sales to its allies were still at prices 30 to 40 percent lower than to the West.)

The biggest increases in trade, and also the biggest payments difficulties, occurred in the case of Poland. It is worth noting that the smaller countries, who perforce rely much more heavily on foreign trade than does the huge Soviet Union, have been repeatedly in trouble with their balance of payments through trying to grow too fast: the "overheating" of the economy, and the resulting rundown in material and currency resources, then compels them to jam on the brakes. There is a sizable literature in the East about this species of fluctuation. A particularly striking example is the policy pursued by the Polish government from 1971 to 1975. For reasons that need not detain us here, after the fall of Gomulka (December 1970) the new Polish leadership under Gierek devised a risky expansionist strategy. (Since they alone undertook such a policy during these years, this suggests a sizable degree of autonomy in the bloc, so far as internal economic policies are concerned.) In the years 1971 to 1975, Poland increased investments by 120 percent, money wages by over 60 percent, keeping the prices of most foodstuffs unaltered. Many of the investments involved the import of Western machinery.

Imports rose very steeply and the deficit with the West mounted very rapidly. Already in 1975 it became necessary to slow down drastically. One cause of Poland's difficulties arises from its policy of heavily subsidizing the price of meat: it still sells at the equivalent in our terms of about 30 to 40 cents a pound in the retail stores; twice the government tried to increase prices, and twice they had to retreat in the face of popular riots, the last time being June 1976. The consequences are a high level of meat consumption, which reduces export possibilities while causing shortages at home, and making it necessary to import grain for feed. Polish peasants–agriculture is still mainly private-peasant agriculture–also keep an unusually large number of horses, and they too eat grain. On the positive side, Poland has benefited from the large increase in coal prices (it is a major exporter), which offset the higher prices it has to pay for oil.

East Germany, Czechoslovakia, and Hungary did not run into debt by adopting "Polish" policies. All had had their payments difficulties, in the sense that their earnings of Western currency had been below the levels required to finance the volume of desired purchases; but they managed to avoid major deficits until the huge rises in world prices, which affected not only oil but most other materials that these countries have to import. It is this sharp adverse movement in terms of trade that was the biggest single factor in causing deficits to develop, and in this respect these countries resembled oil-importing Western countries. Since the West was willing to extend credits, there was an increase in indebtedness. Bulgaria's debt does owe something to expansionist domestic policies, since, though without oil, Bulgaria exports primary products; being a small and still underdeveloped country, Bulgaria is among the most vulnerable and faces considerable payments difficulties at present. The healthiest position, relatively, is that of Romania, which is self-sufficient in oil.

The table highlights an interesting contrast: following the huge rise in their imports from the West in 1974, the Eastern countries cut down very severely on this increase after 1974, with the prominent exception of the Soviet Union, whose imports continued to rise very rapidly in 1975, and even, though at a somewhat slower pace, in 1976. Borrowing has continued.

In 1977 the Soviet Union succeeded in considerably reducing its deficit with the West. This was facilitated by a sharp cut in imports of grain from the United States and Canada, following the good harvest of 1976. In the period January to September 1977, the excess of imports from "developed capitalist countries" over exports came to only 1,172 million foreign-trade rubles, against 2,521 million in the same period in 1976. While imports fell, exports rose by 11 percent. However, the disappointing grain harvest of 1977 has been followed by a renewed upswing in grain purchases, which could create problems in 1978.

III. CREDITS AND INDEBTEDNESS

The following table represents estimates of "Eastern" debt. In view of the very many different ways in which loans, credits, etc., are obtained, the figures cannot pretend to be accurate. One source of doubt arises from the fact that a line of credit can be opened (e.g., by Great Britain to the Soviet Union) but only drawn upon over a period of years, with the possibility either of omission or of double-counting. However, the orders of magnitude seem about right.

At first most of these debts were supplier credits, but these have been rapidly overtaken by official export credits on signed contracts and private credits from Western banks, including Eurodollar loans. If ten years ago anyone had suggested that Western countries, firms, and banks would lend even a quarter of such a sum to the East, he might well have seemed to need the services of a psychiatrist. Some reasons for a change in Western attitudes have already been mentioned. To these must be added one more very important point reflected in the fact that the international banking system is responsible for an increasing share in the credits and loans: this is the role of petrodollars–oil money that piles up in the banking centers of the capitalist world and seeks a use. Recession diminished investment opportunities in the West. So by various channels, oil money has helped to finance the Soviet bloc's borrowings. Here is how a UN agency (United Nations

TABLE 3
Comecon Debts to the West ($ billion at year ends)

	1974	1975	1976*
Bulgaria	1.7	2.4	2.8
Czechoslovakia	1.1	1.5	2.1
East Germany	3.6	4.9	5.8
Hungary	2.3	3.2	3.5
Poland	4.9	7.8	10.4
Romania	2.4	2.8	2.8
Soviet Union	5.9	11.4	14.4
Comecon banks	2.1	2.8	3.5
Gross debt	24	36.8	45.3
Deposits with Western banks	6.2	6.6	6
NET DEBT	17.8	30.2	39.3

*Preliminary estimates

Source: **Financial Times,** London, 5 May 1977, based on the work of R. Portes (University of London).

Economic Commission on Europe, 1976a: 101) describes what has occurred and is likely to occur:

> Oil exporters deposit their surpluses in Western banks, a part of these surpluses is re-lent to Eastern countries, which is used to finance their deficits with Western countries. Now, direct links are being established with oil-exporting countries. East European countries borrow from oil exporters for the construction of enterprises at home and credits will be repaid by future products of these enterprises. Or they participate in investment projects (including deliveries of machinery) in oil-producing countries, for part of which they are paid cash. Finally Eastern countries can use these proceeds to finance deficits with Western countries.

Recent examples of deals with oil-producing countries are credits from Iran to the Soviet Union and Poland, to be repaid by deliveries of paper and processed food, and Kuwaiti credits for Romania, paid for in chemicals (United Nations Economic Commission on Europe, 1976b: 130).

Should the startlingly high rate of increase in Eastern borrowing cause concern? Let us first look at the economics, then at the politics.

A great deal of business is done on the basis of long-term credits, especially if sales of capital goods are concerned. Many countries have schemes under which export credits are guaranteed by government, as part of general plans to encourage exporters and to make them more competitive. The result is that many credits are offered at rates of interest that are below the normal market rate. These procedures have not been designed with Eastern countries in mind, but they benefit from them because, given their excellent record of punctual repayment, they are usually given the treatment accorded to those with the highest credit rating. It is true that, having reneged on debts inherited from previous regimes, the communists have been most careful to honor their obligations (even where, as we have seen, it has been necessary to starve their own people to export food). The only exception so far is North Korea, whose megalomaniac leader, Kim Il Sung, is perhaps to be treated as a special case. Therefore, so far, banks and other credit institutions have been ready to lend, or to guarantee loans. There have also been some important banking operations in the Eurodollar market conducted by the communists themselves, either through banks they control in the West (e.g., the Moscow Narodny Bank, based in London), or through Comecon banks. The Federal Import-Export agency was prevented by Congress from acting as other similar agencies in the West have acted.

Has this gone too far for *economic* grounds? Ought our capital not be used for better purposes than to strengthen the communist economies? We should be clear that we are not subsidizing them, or, if we are, to no greater extent than any of our other credit-worthy customers of capital goods.

One way of looking at things is to relate debt service to export earnings, also taking into account future export earnings. This last point is of obvious importance. Thus Poland incurred substantial debts in the process of re-equipping her industries with Western machinery, with the aim of expanding sales of manufactures to the West made by this machinery. Soviet raw material and fuel reserves are vast; her debt is still a small fraction of her national product, and insofar as the equipment bought on credit is used to expand production, the means of repayments are being created by the credits themselves. Indeed, some of the credits, as we shall see, specifically provide for such repayment, as when West German pipe is to be paid for by the natural gas that will flow through it. Of course, the relative advantage of such a deal depends not only on interest rates but also on relative prices. In this, as in all other such cases, no conclusion can be reached without a careful study of the terms of any deal. It must be supposed that the Western business partner has satisfied himself that the deal is profitable. It would plainly be childish simply to assert that the borrower benefits. Of course he does, or he would not borrow. But the world has seen many a highly prosperous moneylender! Most economic transactions voluntarily entered into must be assumed to benefit both parties.

However, the question remains: have things gone too far? In the case of Poland, this may well be so. It seems that the debt service is above 30 percent of the value of exports to the West (a much lower percentage of *total* exports, of course). Relative to the size of the economy, Poland's debts are the highest. Past experience does not suggest that the Poles will have the managerial, technical, and marketing skill to expand greatly their sales of manufactures to the West. Agricultural exports are limited both by Poland's own farm output and by the restrictions imposed (on all outsiders) by the Common Market's agricultural policy. In recent years Poland's dependence on imported grain has substantially increased.

But even apart from Poland's vulnerable position (complicated by a shaky internal political situation), there is likely to be some reduction in the willingness of Western financial institutions to lend on a large scale. Indeed, there is also a reluctance in the East to incur such large debts, and therefore a tendency—to be examined later—to cut down the import bill and push exports.

What of the *politics* of lending? There are several possible attitudes one could take.

The first bases itself on the notion that capital is scarce, that it could be used at home, or lent to developing countries, that its commitment to communist countries shows the wrong sense of priorities. This would indeed be so if in fact the money lent, or credits given, to the East were for that reason unavailable to domestic borrowers or a Third World country. This is difficult to document. True enough, places such as Bangladesh need capital, but in the form of aid, since commercial opportunities there are limited and the risk high. Successful Third World countries such as Singapore, Taiwan, and Brazil, have no difficulty in attracting Western capital. Also it must be remembered that productive capacity is specific; by this I mean that the sort of things the Soviet Union obtains on credit (oil equipment, say, or pipelines, or timber-cutting machinery) may have no alternative use. *These* specific goods may simply not be wanted in Bangladesh or, for that matter, in Baltimore.

The second point is much more serious, and depends on a particular interpretation of Soviet policy objectives, a matter of fundamental importance that will recur again in this paper. Whether or not Moscow aims for "world conquest," and whether or not the word "aims" has operational meaning,[1] the fact remains that the Soviet Union and the West are in a state of conflict, of world-wide competition, détente or no détente. The political atmosphere may become highly charged, and even if the unthinkable nuclear confrontation remains unthinkable, relations may become strained or even broken off, with both sides striving to do each other economic harm, ignoring contracts and commercial obligations. (It may perhaps have been forgotten that the *West* broke many contracts when imposing embargoes in the years of the cold war.) Within such a scenario, loans of $40 billion (which some consider will be $60 billion by the end of the decade) may represent money lost, productive capacity created with credits that will not be repaid, uncollectable debts. Some put matters even more strongly and, in the words of one cynical Hungarian, point out that the Soviets always either pay you punctually or come and take you over. The past record certainly does not suggest that the Soviet Union would default as a matter of policy intention. Indeed no such intention need be assumed. It is just that if relations become seriously strained, for whatever reason, say through the uncontrollable actions of third parties in the Middle East, the material counterpart of the credits would be in Soviet hands.

The third argument points in a different direction. It stresses the fact that, through these credits, the Soviet Union and her allies are brought more closely into world trade, their economies geared in to a greater extent to the economies of the West. There would therefore be a loss if these relations are disrupted, and this might serve to deter political action that would cause such disruption. The argument relates to trade links in general and their consequences. In practice, many foreign credits give rise to more interdependence rather than more autarky: there is need for spares, replacements, the more up-to-date versions of what has been bought, and so on. Thus the very large purchases of machinery and equipment by the East in the last five years have not led to any reduction in demand, but rather the contrary (though balance of payments reasons may compel a temporary cutback). Take as a different example the credits that have helped develop the Soviet gas industry and its pipelines. This development establishes a solid lodgment in the West German fuel market, and must give rise to expectations of major purchases of many kinds of German machinery with the hard currency earned (over and above the gas deliveries required to repay credits). Default on political grounds would not only put a stop to German machinery deliveries, but would leave the Soviet Union with gas and a pipeline with perhaps no alternative use. I am not suggesting that such considerations would transform Soviet foreign policy. They may, nonetheless, be a significant contributory element in policy discussions.

There remains the point that credits assist the Soviet Union indirectly, to maintain and increase her levels of military spending. This, and the fact that the machines bought on credit strengthen the Soviet Union generally, will be discussed later, when we come to the general issues of the politics of trade.

East-West Trade: Its Relative Importance

It has been argued in the London *Times* that, since trade with the West plays a much bigger role in the East than trade with the East does in the West, they gain more than we do from it. The facts are as stated; but the conclusion drawn is odd. The facts first. In 1975, the East took 0.8 percent of U.S. exports, 2.8 percent of British exports, 3.1 percent of French exports. Only Finland and Austria can be said to be seriously dependent on trade with the East. By contrast, the European Comecon countries took 37 percent of their imports from the West, and supplied 28 percent of their exports to the West (United Nations, 1976a: 64).[2]

This is the inevitable consequence of the West's quantitative dominance in world trade, much of which consists of exchanges *between* Western countries. Why do I say that the conclusion is odd? Well, let us apply this logic. Suppose one were to say: trade with the United States forms a larger percentage of the foreign trade of Canada or Mexico than trade with Canada or Mexico does of that of the United States, and that therefore they gain more from such trade than the United States. We would surely all demur from such a conclusion. The advantages or disadvantages relate to the actual trade deals, and cannot be affected by what percentage they represent in a given country's total trade turnover.

It is a different matter if one is measuring not relative advantage but vulnerability. However, as far as the Soviet Union is concerned one must not forget that her *total* trade represents only five to six percent of her national product, and that total imports of machinery and equipment from the West are certainly less than this if expressed as a percentage of all machinery installed in the Soviet Union in any recent year. The bulk of it is, of course, Soviet-made.

This reasoning, however, would be misleading. Just as in certain items the role of Comecon partners is very important indeed (for instance in the supply of cranes, ships, and railroad equipment), so Western technology and know-how is of major significance in certain branches of industry: electrical engineering, chemical machinery (especially for synthetics), motor vehicle production, and so on. The Soviet Union is now urgently in need of oil-drilling equipment usable in Siberian conditions, and imports pipe on a massive scale. The planners must be well aware that there is a technology gap that affects their allies too: Comecon countries too often supply each other with various kinds of obsolete machines, which looks good in trade statistics, but does not greatly help efficiency. Then there is the dependence on the West for grain, and for other items temporarily short. In other words, the Soviet planners have come to rely on the West for some key items, but in aggregate these items represent a modest proportion of the total output of the Soviet Union.

It is quite another matter with the other Eastern countries. Trade is overwhelmingly important for countries such as Czechoslovakia and Hungary, for instance—with the West playing a large role—and in the case of Romania, trade with the West has increased particularly rapidly and has almost equalled her trade with Comecon partners in 1975. Soviet and Western attitudes toward these facts can appear confused, because they are contradictory. Thus the Soviet Union would prefer Comecon countries to be dependent on Soviet supplies, but some of these supplies can be sold to the West for hard currency, which is good for the Soviet balance of payments; so that at times it "pays" to compel her Comecon allies to rely more on trade with the West (or, in the case of oil, the Arab states). The smaller countries themselves are, in varying degrees, very willing to diversify, so as not to be too dependent on Moscow. Western attitudes are sometimes influenced by the desirability of encouraging this greater independence from Moscow, and this has led to more favorable treatment for certain Eastern countries than for the Soviet Union.

IV. PROSPECTS FOR TRADE

The recent upsurge in Eastern imports from the West has outrun their ability to pay, and therefore we are bound to see in the very short run a check in the upward trend of Western sales to the East. This, however, is not a forecast, just an instantaneous photograph of the present situation. Let us look ahead at prospects and trends. Before examining the political desiderata, which undoubtedly have affected and will affect the outcome, let us look more closely at the commercial prospects.

Expansion of trade is held back primarily by the volume and value of Eastern sales to the West. Clearly, they have a long "shopping list" of goods which, for balance-of-payments reasons, they cannot afford to buy. Furthermore, there is the need to service their debt, to repay credits. Therefore the key constraint is their ability to sell more to the West. It has to be to the *West,* because their surpluses and deficits with each other, apart from cancelling out, are not convertible into Western currencies (save for a very limited extent), and the same is true of much of their trade with developing countries. It may be worth remarking on this point that the Soviet Union appears, according to its trade accounts, to have a sizable surplus with developing countries, but on closer examination this surplus becomes either mythical or mysterious: the Soviet Union has no overall surplus with the countries actually listed in her trade accounts–and the list is virtually exhaustive–but an amount well in excess of $1 billion is exported to no country at all (i.e., appears in the total sales to the category "developing countries," but is not attributed to any country). The probability is that these are arms sales, clumsily concealed as to their destination. Some of these *may* be paid for in hard currency, but more probably they are provided in the form of aid, with repayment in goods over a period of years, if at all.

Let us return to "Eastern" exports to the West and examine for a moment their composition.

One is struck by the dominance, in the case of Soviet exports, of fuel and raw materials (and indeed most of the "basic manufactures" are processed materials). In other words, the trade is traditional, with Soviet trade following the pattern typical of

TABLE 4
Western Imports from the East, c.i.f.

	Value–$ million 1975	
	Total	**Soviet Union**
All Western industrial countries –Total	19,650	9,599
Food and live animals	1,732	152
Beverages and tobacco	125	14
Crude materials (excluding fuels)	3,005	2,130
Mineral fuels, etc.	6,850	4,880
Animal and vegetable oils and fats	290	150
Chemicals	1,034	345
Basic manufactures	3,276	1,330
Machinery and transport equipment	1,841	486
Miscellaneous manufactured articles	1,377	66
Goods not classified by kind	120	46

Source: United Nations Economic Commission for Europe, 1976a: 85.

developing countries and indeed of Tsarist Russia: exports of primary products, imports of highly fabricated goods, especially machinery. The one departure from the traditional pattern is grain: in 1913 Russia was a big exporter, whereas now she has become an importer on a formidable scale, with consequences to be examined in a moment.

Yet the Soviet Union is, according to her own claims, the world's second largest industrial producer, soon to catch up with the United States in total output. Why, then, cannot she expand sales of manufactured goods?

Soviet spokesmen complain of discriminatory restrictions and prejudice, but privately they would doubtless agree that these are not major factors (though they are certainly not insignificant). One can see this by studying the performance of Soviet exports in those markets (Sweden, for instance) which are open to them free of any discriminatory restrictions. Only in Finland have they made serious headway, but the Finns are in a delicate political position and feel under some obligation to facilitate Soviet sales, despite complaints from some of their businessmen.

The basic problems are, in a sentence, quality, service, and marketing. Soviet consumer goods are, with few exceptions, mediocre, poorly designed, and out of date, as any visitor to the Soviet Union can see for himself. Let him try a simple test: do *not* go to the *Beryozka* shops, where specially selected and scarce goods of superior quality are sold for dollars, and try instead to find in the normal stores *any* item worth buying to take home. The task is not impossible, but it is difficult, reflecting the fact that the mass-production goods made for the Soviet market tend to be inferior, and virtually unsaleable in the West. This is obvious in the case of clothing. Consumer durables are often defective and almost always of obsolete design. There are exceptions, of course: Soviet watches, radios, and cameras sell in Great Britain, for instance, and the Soviet Fiat car is being marketed under the name *Lada*. But these do not amount to large sums. Similarly, even a trebling of vodka exports would represent only a drop in the ocean in balance-of-payments terms, and as for caviar, the Soviet Union imports more than she exports, because of shortage of Soviet sturgeon (it is not that they voted with their fins for

Iranian capitalism, but the Iranian shores of the Caspian are less polluted, and less affected by hydro-electric dams and irrigation works on river estuaries).

This brings us to machinery and equipment. There are some Soviet products that can compete in world markets, but in general it is agreed that Soviet machinery tends to be below commonly accepted international standards. For a generation their designers concentrated on standardized and cheap machine-tools, and a number of analysts have pointed out that Soviet equipment is relatively cheap, comparing internal ruble prices and costs with those in the outside world. Yet, cheap or not, it does not sell. Again, the complaint is that the equipment is out of date, in some cases clumsy in use, and also that after-sales service and supplies of spares are bad (they are bad also in the Soviet Union itself for Soviet machinery, as innumerable complaints show). The Soviet Union is an importer of technology from the West precisely because (or largely because) of the backwardness of her own machinery industry—backwardness in quality, not quantity.

Even where the Soviet Union is in the forefront of technological progress, the export results have been small. One reason is that some of the biggest progress has been in the defense sector, and such goods are not exported, at least not to the West (any more than we export nuclear submarines to the Soviet Union!). But observe the Soviet record in civilian aircraft: they have good designs, their jet planes and engines are regarded as impressive by experts, but one virtually never sees a Soviet-made airliner except in a communist country, or unless it is supplied under an aid scheme. The problem seems to be that it is not economic in use.

The final item on the list of obstacles is poor marketing. Here one must refer again to the state monopoly on foreign trade and the barrier this erects between the Soviet production managers and design teams on the one hand, and Western markets on the other. The Soviets lack not only direct personal contact, but have frequently had no access to journals and catalogues. The less prestigious research institutes suffer by being cut off from human contact abroad. In the complex area of product design and marketing, the state trading corporations lack expertise and flexibility. But there is another point of importance: Soviet enterprise management and design bureaus are unaccustomed to having to serve the consumers' needs in a competitive economic environment. Within their own country they are in a monopoly situation, not merely because only state enterprises exist and imports are strictly controlled, but because competition between Soviet state enterprises is eliminated by the system of administrative allocation, which ties the supplier to the customer and the customer to the supplier. Selling is hardly ever a problem for the Soviet manager; he has sleepless nights over supplies and procurements (plan or no plan, materials may not arrive in time). The design bureaus are dominated by scientists and engineers, and pay too little attention to economy in use. It is difficult to see how these faults can be remedied without major changes in the system of planning and management.

The Soviet leaders are aware of all this. Indeed Kosygin, in his speech to the 25th Party Congress, referred to a proposal to set up industrial enterprises specializing in export production. However, the Soviet political-economic establishment is set in its ways and intensely conservative and reform-resistant. One must anticipate that progress will not be rapid.

This leaves us with the traditional raw materials and fuels. The Soviet Union can develop exports of iron ore, perhaps also copper and some other metals, if the rich deposits in remote Siberian areas can be brought into production, a task which is expensive in time and effort. Timber exports will surely not expand rapidly: plans are seldom fulfilled, production grows slowly, the Soviets' own demand is not fully met. The most promising lines in the short run are certainly oil and natural gas. Increased sales—and especially higher prices—of these two items have very greatly helped the Soviet balance of payments with the West in recent years, and exports are still rising. The bigger Western markets in 1976 were Italy, West Germany, France, Finland, and Great Britain.

But around oil there hangs a large question mark. The plan for 1980 envisages a total oil output of about 640 million tons, which is 12.7 million barrels a day. The CIA does not consider this feasible, and has published estimates ranging from 11.8 to

11.0 million barrels roughly 60 million tons below the planned target. Its reasoning: the exhaustion of the older oilfields, and the difficulties faced in bringing into operation the oilfields located in remote northwest Siberian areas, in very harsh climatic conditions. Also it is said that exploration and new drilling are backward, as is the technology (the Soviets are, however, trying to make good the latter by imports). Output will fall absolutely after 1980, according to the CIA's controversial report.

If the CIA is right, the Soviet trade planners face a harsh dilemma. Despite some efforts to damp down the growth of oil utilization in the Soviet Union (e.g., by using less oil for generation of electricity), demand is rising. Even more rapid is the increase in demand from other Comecon countries, especially as they are becoming rapidly motorized (there are quite substantial socialist traffic snarl-ups in Budapest, for instance). The present plan envisages total oil exports to Comecon countries of 364 million tons of oil in the five years 1976 to 1980, which is hardly consistent with the CIA forecast, which implies an oil deficit for Comecon as a whole by 1980, and an even worse one by 1985 (i.e., then Soviet exports would be smaller than the imports of other Comecon countries).

But *is* the CIA right? Taking the risk of being proved wrong, let me express doubts, reinforced by the views of the author of a thesis on the Soviet oil industry and by my own knowledge that the plan-fulfillment record of that industry in the past has been unusually good. True enough, the last five-year plan was underfulfilled, but this was by 10 million tons, not 60, and was due not to failures in drilling the oil-wells but to delays in constructing various processing and transport facilities. The plan through the first half of 1977 is up to schedule. The priority of oil is high, precisely because the Soviet planners know its importance for their balance of payments and that of their allies. Experience shows that estimates of future oil production are apt to be falsified, but this is true of the CIA estimate too, and most errors of Western estimates in the past have been *underestimates.* Let me assert that the CIA will, in this instance, be proved wrong, that the 1980 plan target will be almost reached, and that output will increase, not diminish, through 1985, though at a decelerating rate.

Even so, the increased level of oil utilization within the Soviet Union and other Comecon countries will severely limit the possible increases in sales to the West. Sales could go up by, say, 10 to 15 percent by 1980, hardly more, and this would compel other Comecon countries to buy some of their oil from the Arabs for hard currency. (It would all be much more difficult still if the CIA were proved right in their more "pessimistic" output forecast.)

Another "unknown" is the price of oil. The Soviet Union gained greatly from the OPEC decision of 1973, and will gain from any future increases, to an extent we can hardly forecast and which cannot be known to the Russians either.

So oil should help, but only to a modest extent. Much more hopeful is the case of natural gas. Vast new fields have been opened up in west Siberia and also in the area north of the Caspian. Pipelines have been built into west-central Europe, and there the gas is all the more welcome because the North Sea gas close to the shores of the Netherlands, which has supplied not only the Netherlands but northwest Germany and Belgium, will soon approach exhaustion. If this happens, the price will rise, and the Soviets will have a good and valuable market for a product that their planning system can handle relatively efficiently (no problems of product design or quality: what goes into the pipeline at one end comes out at the other). In terms of percentage, this may prove to be the most rapidly increasing Soviet export in the next decade. However, it is easy to see that oil is a far larger item: a doubling of natural gas exports over its 1975 levels would yield 450 million rubles, much less than the proceeds of a 10 percent rise in sales of oil and oil products. There are good long-term prospects for nonferrous metals, for instance the vast Udokan deposits in east Siberia. Mining these may require deliveries of Western equipment, but in any case results cannot be produced until the 1980s. In the short run there are shortages, which probably helps to explain the sudden disappearance of nonferrous metals from published trade statistics for 1976.

Soviet efforts to sell more to the West, while repaying past credits, will face obstacles, and the balance-of-payments situation should be tight for the next few years at least, compelling the

Soviet Union to hold back further increases in imports. The extent to which this will prove necessary would depend to a great degree on the extent to which the oil industry fulfills its plans, and also on the movements of prices of this and other products.

Soviet ability to pay for imports of technology and other manufactures depends on one other variable: the need to import grain. This may be seen if one looks at the trade consequences of the bad grain harvest of 1975. One has only to look at the pattern of trade with the United States and Canada in this and the following year (see Table 5).

Here is concentrated over half of the Soviet Union's dollar and hard-currency deficit. Since Soviet exports to the United States and Canada have been and remain small, this deficit has to be covered by surpluses with other Western countries' credits and gold sales. This "grain-induced" deficit clearly diminishes the Soviet Union's disposable stocks of dollars. It could be reduced if the Soviet Union could cope with its grain problem.

Why *this* problem? This is no place for a detailed analysis of Soviet agriculture. It is the subject of bitter jests in the Soviet Union itself: "If we collectivize the Sahara, very soon they will be importing sand." The truth is perhaps more prosaic. After neglect under Stalin, the Soviet leadership in the last 20 years

TABLE 5
Soviet Imports and Exports with U.S. and Canada
(millions of rubles)

	1975	1976
Total Imports from U.S.	1,462.1	2,006.8
Grain Imports from U.S.	843.0	1,185.0
Exports to U.S.	137.4	198.7
Total Imports from Canada	439.3	499.3
Grain Imports from Canada	380.8*	440.9*
Exports to Canada	31.9	41.9

*including flour

Source: Soviet trade accounts, 1976.

has done much, and spent much, to raise agricultural productivity. There have been very large investments, and the incomes of peasants have been greatly raised from miserably low levels. The result is by no means discreditable: output has risen, grain harvests average about 50 percent above the levels of the 1950s. This advance has been achieved at very high cost. Productivity has risen, but remains low, lower than other Comecon countries, let along the West. Reasons include an unfavorable soil and climate, which is not the Soviet government's fault, but also bureaucratic planning, large impersonal farms, poor quality of machinery, lack of roads and of transport facilities, and a negative attitude of the peasants toward their work. The risk of drought causes substantial variations in harvests between good and bad years. Thus the disaster of 1975 (138 million tons of grain) was followed by a record 1976 (224 million tons). In a highly favorable weather year such as 1976, the Soviet Union can more or less cover its grain needs, but in an average year things become difficult; and when bad weather hits, the Soviet Union becomes suddenly the world's largest importer of grain, as American farmers and the world grain traders well know.

Yet it may be asked: surely there were bad years as well as good before 1963 (the first year of major purchases in the West), and grain harvests are now on average much higher. So there must be another reason for the high level of imports. Actually there are two. One is that under Stalin people just went hungry when the harvest failed, whereas Khrushchev had, and Brezhnev has, a different attitude and also a different problem: Stalin could terrify people into silence; *they* need popular acquiescence. The second reason is that there is now a much higher livestock population, and, as in Poland, a retail price for meat kept low by a huge subsidy. Demand exceeds supply. Efforts are made to build up livestock herds. They need feed grain. It is this attempt to improve the over-starchy diet of the population, and to match Western consumption standards for meat, which greatly increases demand for grain, especially as yields of other feed crops and of hay are poor.

Of course the Soviet planners do not expect to have to continue to import the huge quantities they purchased in the 1975-

1976 agricultural year. But in a run of normal-weather years there will still surely be net imports, and this is clearly also the Soviet expectation, as emerges from the negotiations over this issue with the United States. If bad-weather luck hits them, they will again be vulnerable, dependent on essential supplies from the West. We will discuss later what practical conclusions it would be proper to draw from this disagreeable (for them) fact.

I shall deal more briefly with the smaller Comecon countries. Two of them, East Germany and Czechoslovakia, are old-established industrial areas, inevitably net importers of raw materials, fuels, and grain, though in fact their agriculture is now impressively productive, despite collectivization. On a slightly lower level of development, but important industrially, are Hungary and Poland. All these four countries obtain most of their materials and fuels from the Soviet Union, in exchange for machinery, equipment, and a wide range of other manufactures. Hungary has an cxport surplus of meat, and Poland has considerable agricultural potential, but exports to Western Europe are impeded by the Common Agricultural Policy administered from Brussels. Taking the four countries together, they are net importers of grain, especially Poland (as already mentioned, this is explained by the large number of horses and the effect of the meat subsidy on demand for feed grain). Poland is exceptional in having a big export surplus of coal, which in fact provided 30 percent of her exports to the West in 1975.

The main chance for these countries to expand their sales to Western markets is, of course, in manufactures. They have made some limited headway. East German cameras and optics have done well, and the special arrangements between the two Germanies have facilitated a notable penetration by East German industrial goods into West European markets. East German quality, if not up to the best Western standards, is certainly well above the Eastern average. This fact remains one that poor workmanship and lack of enterprise are not due only to the inefficient nature of the system. The Soviet-type economy operated by Germans is evidently more productive than the Soviet-type economy operated by the Russians. Indeed, in the Soviet Union itself, standards and quality are higher in the Baltic republics, whose people have had a different tradition and experience, than in Russia proper, let alone Central Asia. It would be very interesting to make a detailed comparison of productivity, quality, and methods of work between East and West Germany, for here at least one would be dealing with the same people. The task is not being attempted here: it would call for a large research team, and has only indirect connection with East-West trade. However, we must take seriously the industrial strength and export capacity of East Germany, even though they are not in the forefront as far as new technology is concerned (if they were, then the Soviet Union would be less dependent on the West for it). Sixty percent of East German exports to the West are to West Germany, under the special intra-German arrangements.

Czechoslovakia too has an industrial tradition. The Czech lands were the center of industrial growth in the Austro-Hungarian empire before World War I. Firms bearing world-famous names such as Skoda and Bata flourished between the wars, and the "bren gun" used by British infantry in World War II had been designed in Brno. But under communist rule quality declined steeply. Efforts were made to make in Czechoslovakia (in small and uneconomic quantities) every type of machine, a form of stupid autarky that affected other Comecon countries too, for reasons to be seen when we discuss the role (in this case lack of role) of Comecon. The nonpriority consumer-goods industries were neglected. As a result (so I was told in Prague) the Czechs began to import shoes from Yugoslavia to stimulate improvement in quality. My Czech colleague exclaimed: "For us in Czechoslovakia to import *shoes* of better quality from *Yugoslavia!!* Bata would turn in his grave, and he would be right!"

Things have improved since the early 1960s, to which time the above remark relates. But it is still very hard for the Czechs to produce enough goods fit for Western markets. In fact their biggest sales have been iron and steel, followed by coal and coke, rather than manufactures. One reason, which applies in some measure to all these countries, must be stressed: in the Comecon area as a whole quality is not high; there is usually a sellers' market, and so it is relatively simple to sell mediocre goods at home or to other Comecon countries, rather than to struggle to sell in difficult and competitive Western markets. One can fulfill output and turnover plans more easily, and indeed make higher profits. So managers lack the goal and the incentive to sell in the West, whatever the wishes of the planners might be.

In several Eastern countries the planners have tried to make selling to the West more advantageous, by a variety of expedients. One is the straightforward method of issuing orders, but, in this area as in most others, the carrot has operational advantages over the stick. There are schemes by which enterprises are allowed to retain a proportion of the convertible currency they earn, partly to pay for imported equipment and partly for more directly pleasant expenditures, such as travel to Western countries. This can be reinforced by expedients such as altering foreign exchange coefficients, so that exports earning Deutschemarks or dollars "count" for more than rubles or zloty (more, that is, than at the official rates). Indeed some countries, notably Poland, have a bewildering array of exchange rates, depending on the nature of the transaction. But they all have a hard task, counteracting the nonmarket nature of their systems, the ease with which management can sell without effort second-class goods. One Eastern economist put it this way: "It is very hard for us to make goods of the necessary quality to sell in the West when it is so easy to sell rubbish to the Soviet Union." We must expect some improvements, but they may well be slow, even though Eastern countries now have the burden of interest and repayment on credits and loans from the West.

Poland had re-equipped half of its industry with Western machinery since 1970, on credit to be sure, but the Poles hoped that this would enable them to export more to the West. It has certainly helped them in exports to Comecon countries: for instance, in Hungary one sees large numbers of Polski Fiat cars, made largely with Italian machinery and know-how. But can they compete with Italian-made Fiats in the West? Surely not. Nonetheless, Polish mining machinery and clothing, to mention two items, have made headway.

Hungary (and to a more limited extent Poland) has been experimenting with greater managerial autonomy, with more stress on the market and on selling, and with much wider contact with Western business. Hungarians are freer to travel than other "Easterners." They have also been in the lead in encouraging *joint ventures* with Western firms and even some limited Western investment and marketing. Thus one can see Shell signs at gas stations; the Intercontinental and Hilton hotels in Budapest have been built with American money; and Hungarian firms make components for assembly in the West (for instance, they make parts for Italian Fiats, as well as those manufactured in the Soviet Union and Poland). Romania even has a law that is supposed to encourage direct investment in Romania by Western capitalists, though it has not yet been followed by action. Joint ventures with Western firms can be expected to yield advantages to all concerned. They provide a market, the exact specifications of the product are determined by the Western partner ("which is very useful information for us, and imposes market discipline upon us," as one of their economists told me). There are also clear advantages for the smaller countries in producing components on a large scale for large outside markets on the basis of long-term contracts. The Western firm benefits from low labor costs and the absence of strikes. Western firms have in fact made "over a thousand agreements on productive cooperation" with the East, confined so far largely to engineering, electronics, and chemicals (Shmelev, 1977: 83).

So we may be seeing Western multinational firms using the smaller Eastern countries for processing and component manufacture, and in this way trade can grow. It is perhaps insufficiently realized how very considerable today is the trade that consists of transfers within the multinational corporation. Of course, the Hungarian or Polish operation will be conducted and owned not by a subsidiary of the Western corporation but by the state. But it could act in a manner closely reminiscent of that of any subcontractor, working for a big Western corporation in, say, Singapore. The Soviet source just quoted considers that inter-firm cooperation can be greatly extended, and that so far Hungary and Poland have made most progress in this.

Another form of joint project is the joint investment, as when the Hungarian firm Csepel joins with the West German Krupps for production of numerically controlled machine tools. The Soviet source deplores the relative backwardness of the Soviet Union in this kind of development, but mentions a recent agreement with France and Sweden to provide automation equipment used in Soviet machine tools that are being exported to the West. France has invested some capital for the Ust-Ilimsk pulp and paper combine, and several Western countries have provided investment resources for the building of the gas pipeline from the Soviet Union to Germany, France, and Austria, and a new pipe from Iran across the Soviet Union (Shmelev, 1977: 83, 87).[3]

I mention these developments here because they could provide a way of enlarging exports of the smaller Eastern countries, thereby enabling them to buy more from the West. As already indicated, closer links with Western economies are welcome to many people in these countries, by no means excluding influential party people. Such developments are tolerated by Moscow, but one has the strong impression that they are not welcome. A Polish official once told me, unofficially, that "it is not possible for us to encourage direct Western investment," and he looked eastwards as he said it. They have to maneuver cautiously. It could be risky to divert to the West resources needed for exports to the Soviet Union or for Comecon-sponsored integration schemes.

A modest increase in sales of manufactures and components to the West seems likely from these countries. However, their balance of payments is and will be under strain for a reason mentioned earlier: the Soviet Union is finding it impossible to increase rapidly enough its deliveries of items of great importance to the economies of its Comecon partners, and the growth of these economies increases their import needs. Oil is only the most obvious and best-known example. A pipeline has already been constructed from the Adriatic to take Middle East oil into Hungary and Czechoslovakia. Several of these countries import grain from the West. These are additional burdens on slender resources of Western currency. It must be noted too that their exports to the oil-producing states have been small, and that to pay for this oil they will need surpluses with other hard-currency countries. All this necessarily sets severe limits on expansion of Western exports to these countries. It sets limits, too, on the possibilities of Comecon integration, of which more in a moment.

One exception must be mentioned. Romania has shown herself politically independent, has avoided major commitments to Comecon, is self-sufficient in oil, grain, and most foods, and has deliberately diverted a large proportion of her trade to the West. Being in the throes of industrialization, Romania needs a wide range of capital goods.

Where Does Comecon Come In?

As already indicated, Comecon led a shadowy existence for the first years of its life. From 1956 it began to be taken seriously, but until very recently it played an insignificant role in East-West trade. Each member-country made its own separate deal with each separate Western country. This may change as and when EEC officials in Brussels succeed in centralizing the Common Market countries' negotiations with the East, since evidently the Soviet Union will not like the Bulgars, Czechs, and Poles making separate agreements with all of Western Europe, and so we may see a Comecon-EEC trade negotiation one day. But we are far from this now. Consequently, one simple and short answer to the question put at the head of this section is: Comecon comes in nowhere. Yet it is of importance to our theme, though to some extent it is an indirect importance.

Until recently, each Comecon country made its own central plan; in the first years they copied the Soviet Union not only in its institutions but also in its degree of self-sufficiency, producing far too great an assortment of products, including machinery, in uneconomically small quantities and duplicating each other. It is only gradually that Comecon institutions began to unravel the muddle. In 1971 an ambitious program of Comecon integration was published. There would be joint long-term planning, many more joint investment prospects, agreements on specialization, and even, in due course, multilateral trade and currency convertibility. The role of Comecon banks was extended, as was the function of the so-called transferable ruble. There was an expansion, too, of sectoral joint planning under such Comecon bodies as Intermetall and Interkhim, for metallurgy and chemicals, respectively. Under Comecon's aegis there were many bilateral agreements signed, so that, as already mentioned, the Soviet Union can rely on supplies of specified equipment, ships, etc., from East Germany, in exchange for iron ore, timber, gas, etc. There have been instances, too, of investments made by one country in another, sometimes with the dispatch of workers and technicians, though this has been on a much smaller scale than the migration of labor in Western Europe.

While Comecon at present concerns East-West trade primarily because its members trade with one another by preference, joint investment projects have been growing in importance, and in some industries there is progress in specialization on production of parts: thus the big new Kama truck plant, which under U.S. equipment and know-how, will comprise numerous components from Comecon countries, including lighting equipment from Czechoslovakia, brakes from Poland, horns from Hungary, repaying in trucks. The Soviet Union also pays Hungary in cars for supplies of components to its Fiat plant, while supplying the Hungarians with gearboxes for *Ikarus* buses, which are delivered to the Soviet Union, and so on. Czech trucks are being assembled in Bulgaria on Czech license and with some Czech-made parts, and so on. The Comecon investment bank has granted credits to Hungary for the expansion of its bus factory. However, the Soviet author of the article from which these facts are taken points out how much more should be done even in car and truck-production planning, where integration has made more progress than elsewhere.

These are all significant developments, but it remains the case that the vast bulk of intra-Comecon trade is conducted on the basis of bilateral barter. Convertibility is formally possible through the Comecon banking system, but is still very limited. Effective joint planning develops slowly. Duplication of investments still occurs. The Western businessman still finds that he deals with the Soviet Union, or Hungary, or Poland, as if Comecon did not exist, and he cannot convert his earnings in zloty or Czech crowns into rubles or forints.

If Comecon were really a joint-planning area, planning for maximizing self-sufficiency, the prospects for East-West trade would be adversely affected. But this is not the case. It may be worth indicating briefly the obstacles to East-East trade, which remain serious.

First and foremost, internal prices in most Comecon countries bear no relationship whatever to the prices (based on world, i.e., capitalist, prices) at which trade occurs, nor are they affected by supply-and-demand or relative scarcity. Furthermore, the availability of goods for export depends on planners' decisions in each country. Exchange rates are unrealistic.

How can one have multilateral trade and convertibility under these conditions? Bilateral balancing ensures an exchange of goods not only of equivalent cash value, but also of equivalent scarcity: from this point of view goods are divided into "hard" and "soft," according to whether they are short or abundant within Comecon. The annual bargaining session between pairs of countries results in a balance of trade by categories of hardness and softness. In general, metal goods, many machines, and nearly all consumer goods are "soft"; food, raw materials, and fuels are "hard." A ruble or zloty balance in the possession, say, of Czechoslovakia or Hungary cannot be converted into "hard" goods, or indeed into any goods, unless the Soviet or Polish planners can be persuaded to allocate these goods to them, which, if the goods are "hard," they will be reluctant to do without a quid pro quo. In some cases, a Comecon country will demand payment in dollars for extremely "hard," scarce goods, over and above a negotiated quota (this is true of Soviet oil sales to Hungary, and of Hungarian meat sales to the Soviet Union; some of these so-called dollar deals are a form of bilateral barter, with a dollar sign).

So long as most Comecon countries have a planning system in which enterprises produce to planners' orders, goods and materials are administratively allocated, and prices do not reflect scarcities or utilities, the effective coordination of Comecon countries' economies logically requires a supranational planning authority, a sort of superstate that would have to be Soviet-controlled, since the Soviet Union is so very much the biggest. On political grounds this is bound to be resisted, and so progress toward integration is very slow. Indeed, several Eastern officials told me that it is easier, once permission has been granted, to buy and sell from and to the West, than to get into the bilateral quota bargaining and bureaucracy of East-East trade.

Obstacles to Trade

Any Eastern trade expert would have interrupted me some time ago: what about obstacles put in the way of trade by the West; what about discriminatory restrictions that make it difficult to sell?

The only obstacle to buying from the West, apart from the problem of paying for these goods, is the COCOM "strategic products" list. This is not now a serious impediment, with some exceptions. Thus a computer system was recently denied them, because of its potential military uses. But even the United States has been less strict in its definitions. Thus not so many years ago the State Department would have judged that heavy trucks have military potential (they could, after all, transport troops and ammunition). Yet now there is American technology and expertise engaged in the Kama project, which will make heavy trucks with the brand-name KAM-AZ.

The obstacle to Eastern exports of *agricultural* produce to Western Europe, their natural market, is "discriminatory" only in the sense that all outsiders are obstructed, including the United States. When Great Britain joined the Common Market and accepted the Common Agricultural Policy, Poland lost an important market for her bacon, for instance, to the advantage of member countries such as Denmark, but so did Canada.

There are other and widespread forms of discrimination which require a closer look. Many countries, including the United States and the EEC countries, deny the Soviet Union and most or all of its allies Most-Favored-Nation (MFN) treatment. This means either that their goods bear higher rates of duty, or they are subject to quantitative restrictions while the same goods from other destinations are free of such restriction, or both at once. This applies to certain goods of Eastern origin and not to others. In addition, powers are sometimes invoked under anti-dumping legislation to prevent large increases in sales of some item or items that are said to be disrupting the market.

A long list of such obstacles can be assembled without difficulty. We must bear in mind that they act as a discouragement to export effort: thus what can be the point of tooling up for an export drive to the West, or of spending money to set up a marketing organization and advertising, if, in the event of success, one will run up against quota restrictions, anti-dumping duties, or other forms of trade barriers?

What is the rationale of Western discriminatory restriction of trade? Politics certainly enters into it as far as the United States is concerned; one has only to look at the debates on the trade bill. Indeed, an informal obstacle to sales of Eastern goods in America is the prejudice or feeling against buying communist-made goods. But there are nonpolitical reasons too, which one can observe in Western Europe.

One is the problem of "meaningful reciprocity." Suppose a Western country grants MFN treatment to the Soviet Union, what can the Soviet Union offer in exchange? What does MFN mean, when the state is the only buyer and import duties are insignificant or nonexistent, and when the decision-making process is hidden from view? Even if the state trading agencies are instructed to behave commercially and to show no discrimination, there is no way of knowing that it is so. In fact we know of instances when it is not so. When the British in 1971 expelled a large number of Soviet diplomats (and trade representatives), Soviet purchases from Britain fell. Conversely, when Brezhnev met the French president, Soviet orders placed in France rose. This can be achieved by a simple (and secret) inter-office memorandum. Then it is the case that Soviet discrimination in favor of Comecon countries is qualitatively different from an EEC customs union: The United States can sell competitively in Western Europe if its goods can overleap the tariff barrier. But Comecon goods obtain administrative preference throughout the East: they will simply not buy from the West if similar goods are obtainable from an Eastern partner.

Furthermore, it is known that Soviet planners, for perfectly understandable reasons, wish to obtain a disposable surplus in trade with some Western countries, in order to use it to buy, for instance, American or Canadian grain, and Malayan rubber. So some Western countries insist on bilateral balancing in the interest of their exporters. If they do, then exporters from *other* Western countries will be handicapped. The same problem arises with specific commodities. Suppose that one country negotiates an import quota for herrings, hats, or haberdashery. Then that country's manufactures of such items have an advantage over those of other countries who have not insisted on a quota.

And how can a Western country demand bilateral balancing of trade, or a quota? By restrictive rules applicable to trade with the East, which can then be the subject of bargaining. To some considerable extent this must be seen as competition *between Western countries* for access to Eastern markets.

The Soviet Union and its allies reply that they provide meaningful reciprocity by buying from the West to the limit of their resources, and that obstruction of their sales has the effect of diminishing their purchases, which is also true. They point out, furthermore, that while a quota for them gives them an *opportunity* to try to sell, a quota granted by them is interpreted as an *obligation* to buy, which is asymmetrical to their detriment. These are matters of systemic misfit, of institutional difference, which do create awkward problems, but these could be overcome with goodwill—which is one of the many points in which politics plays a role. It is also noteworthy that some countries do give MFN treatment and do not discriminate—Canada, for instance, or Sweden (or indeed Great Britain before the war), and no untoward consequences followed. As already argued, there is *not* a superabundance of suitable goods to offer, anyhow. My own view is that we may be being overcautious. The recent shift to Brussels of decision-making on these matters, formerly handled exclusively by separate West European countries, may have the effect of further trade restriction, unless negotiations between EEC and Comecon are seriously started and reach a conclusion. There is no sign of this as of now. (Matters were not helped by a reluctance of Moscow until very recently to "recognize" the European Economic Community.)

Another cause of Western concern is dumping. The argument is based upon the observable fact that Eastern trading organs sell at prices that seem to bear no relation to internal prices and costs. They are under orders to sell at any price (the best price) they can get. A few extremists think that this is done deliberately to disrupt capitalism, but most serious opinion discounts such an interpretation. The facts fit a much less dramatic view. If Polish sandals, Czech cars, Romanian trousers or whatever sell in Britain at very low prices, this is because the British wholesalers have been hard bargainers, not because the Poles, Czechs, and Romanians would not have gladly settled for higher prices! When Soviet ships undercut Western freight rates, they do so to get into the market. If they are eventually offered a share at the higher "conference rates," past experience suggests that they will agree.

A defense against disruptive dumping, whatever its motive, is needed, and the need is understood by the East: I myself heard Mikoyan say so.[4] However, we really must appreciate that dumping is a common occurrence far to the West of the borders of the Soviet empire. Every time the United States sells agricultural surpluses below the domestic farm support price, it is technically engaged in dumping. The same is true when the EEC disposes of some part of its butter or beef mountain. It recently sold great quantities of butter *to the Soviet Union* at a small fraction of the price paid to the producers or charged to West European consumers. Needless to say, the Soviet Union did not complain of dumping! It was glad to buy cheap. In this respect, if in no other, it may be economically more rational than we are. To buy cheap is, after all, usually regarded as wise rather than unwise.

Then there is the irritating Soviet habit, which has been growing, of linking a processing deal with an undertaking by the Western firm concerned to sell Soviet goods of the same value, in a species of barter deal. This has evident convenience for the Soviet planners: it copes with the foreign currency problem, it transfers the task of marketing to the Western firm (and we have seen that marketing is a Soviet weakness). But from the Western viewpoint this is not, or may not be, at all desirable. The firm in question may not wish, or be equipped, to market a miscellany of Soviet goods. Furthermore, by being compelled to do it as part of the process of getting paid, it may be forced to sell these goods in direct competition with domestic producers. Such a deal makes better sense for the Western country if the counterpart is a material or fuel of which the country stands in need: oil or timber, for example, for a West European country or for Japan.

Another difficulty in trade with the East relates to possible large and unpredictable changes in purchasing policy, which may be due to natural causes (such as a drought), or to altered political-economic priorities. There is no meaningful way of studying the Eastern market, because there is, in a sense, no market to study. Whereas an Eastern business executive can visit, negotiate, analyze, advertise, and then (unless prevented by quantitative restrictions) have a reasonable hope of selling, his Western counterpart is much more limited. Of course he can try to predict purchasing requirements by examining published plans: thus if the Soviets decide to double the size of some given industry, offers of machinery used by that industry may well produce results. It was also sensible to take advantage of the urgent need to build and equip new hotels in Moscow and to train staff for them, in time for the 1980 Olympics, and the French have been quick to do this. But suppose we visited the Soviet Union and found that their clothing industry was deplorable, which it is. Would this enable us to sell men's suits, women's dresses, or button-holding machines? Not at all—unless the top planners suddenly decided (at long last!) to do something about Soviet clothing. In other words, what has to be studied is not so much the market as official priorities. Even then we may go wrong. Thus priority is being given to agriculture, but imports of agricultural equipment have remained at a low level; it has evidently been decided to cope with the problem by using Soviet resources. Until recently it was very difficult to open an office in Moscow, or to make contact with industrial ministries. It is still difficult. Some other Eastern countries are much more open in these matters, Hungary for instance.

There are suspicions, mostly unfounded, that the Soviets might purchase prototypes and then make their own products, or that they will ignore patent rights, or pass them on to allies. In fact, the Soviets have tended to be punctilious about patents, and fears of copying miss the point. To take two examples, there was nothing to prevent the Soviet Union from purchasing a small Fiat car or a large Mack truck and copying them. Why, then, did they spend large sums on acquiring machinery, experts, and know-how from Italy and America? What the Soviets need most is production-engineering know-how.

Of course, some Western businessmen have made high profits from East-West trade. But dealing with Eastern trading monopolies requires specialized knowledge, patience in the face of frustration and delay, and great care in negotiating contracts. Some are much more astute than others; experiences differ widely. Certain trading organizations of some Eastern countries (not, one gathers, the Soviet Union) are liable to be corrupt, and cannot be circumvented because of their monopoly position.

A Soviet economist, Shmelev (1977: 84), has included on his list of obstacles to trade not only the usual references to Western discrimination, but also

> insufficient flexibility in relations, especially at microeconomic levels. A negative factor is also the long period spent on negotiating cooperation agreements. For example, according to certain expert assessments, the long delays in negotiation cause Western firms to increase the cost of the contract by 10-20 percent to compensate for losses due to this cause.

This is one example among many of their consciousness of the clumsiness of their own trading arrangements. It is also worth mentioning that, far from regarding the state monopoly as giving a bargaining advantage to the Eastern side, Shmelev (1977: 87) made the following observation:

> East-West cooperation would gain if the various Comecon countries engaged in joint projects with large Western firms associated in other socialist states. . . . At present one sometimes observes imbalance in the economic potential of the partners when on one side there are large corporations and on the other—relatively small enterprises of a number of socialist countries.[5]

In general, one is dealing with a very different system, and it is not entirely inappropriate to cite a saying to the effect that trade between the two systems is analagous to an affair between an elephant and a whale, each of which is accustomed to operating in its own element.

V. THE POLITICAL PERSPECTIVE

Who Gains?

It is said, "Détente is a one-way street." In terms of world politics or military strategy this may or may not be so; it is outside the purview of this paper. But it is often asserted that the Soviets gain more than we do from trade, in some sense at our expense. Let us examine this proposition, before going on to discuss the relationship between trade, détente and politics.

First of all, how does one discover who gains more? There exists a school of thought that the capitalist West gains in its trade with the developing world through so-called "unequal exchange." I asked one enthusiastic Marxist: "Since for something to be unequal one must have some notion of what is equal: what would you regard as *equal* exchange?" The comrade, more enthusiastic than wise, promptly accused me of bourgeois modes of thought. So, returning to our subject, how does one measure relative gain from trade?

It must be accepted, of course, that the Soviet Union and its allies do gain. This has always been taken as a natural cause and consequence of all trade deals voluntarily entered into, barring major errors and miscalculations. But both theory and practice teach us that, of the two parties to a deal, one *may* gain more than the other, and that skill and weight in the process of bargaining can make a difference.

Thus, to take an instance of what appears to be a Soviet coup, the so-called "great grain robbery" of 1972, the Soviet buyers were able to maneuver skillfully and to buy grain at a lower price than a coordinated American negotiating team would have been able to obtain. Accepting that this was so, is there any reason to suppose that this is in any way typical of East-West trade? We have already noted the bureaucratic inflexibilities typical of Eastern trading corporations, noting also the long-established skills of the Russians in the grain and timber markets. Many analysts have observed that the Eastern countries usually sell their goods somewhat *below* world prices, and attribute this to two reasons: the need to counteract prejudice against communist goods, and, more important, weakness or ignorance in bargaining. Indeed we have just noted that "dumping" is often the result of having been beaten down to a lower price. There is no evidence that the Soviets are able habitually to obtain Western goods at below world prices, except for some surplus agricultural products, though they can certainly be hard bargainers and the Western businessmen concerned have on occasion found that profits were few; this was, I understand, the case with the Fiat deal. However, such disappointments are not rare in international business, and I have yet to hear that they are more frequent in East-West trade than elsewhere.

More sophisticated, and more difficult to evaluate, is the argument that their planning priorities, and the way they fit imports into them, ensure that they obtain greater advantage from trade than we do, in the sense of enhanced national economic power. This view rests on the notion that their planners use their imports deliberately to strengthen their economy, especially by modernizing their technology and productive apparatus, whereas in our unplanned system we could be acquiring in exchange all sorts of relative inessentials, such as gasoline for car travel, iron ore which will end up as domestic refrigerators, Bulgarian wine, East German cameras, Soviet timber which will become furniture, and so on. Peter Wiles has argued that machinery and technology are special, that they have a kind of multiplier effect in the country that acquires them, which makes them automatically of greater value than any commodity for which they may be exchanged, apparently regardless of the price.

Frankly, I regard such logic with considerable suspicion. If a British machine tool is exchanged for Indian tea or Brazilian coffee, can we really say that Brazil or India have gained relatively? Of course, tea and coffee have both multiplied in price since 1973, but that does not affect the principle. One is hard put to find a special economic status for machines as such. If West Germany sells to Russia machinery for making synthetic fibers in exchange for oil, this of itself tells us nothing about relative gains. It is true that Soviet planners try to buy only those items that strengthen their economy and society, and we have no mechanism by which we can do this consciously. Or rather our system is based on the assumption that what is profitable to import is what society needs, with occasional exceptions for things such as heroin. This is true, indeed, of our entire economy: *we* tend to leave it to private enterprise to produce and buy and sell in response to the profit motive, while *they* purport to plan for the good of society. *They* claim that this is a source of superiority. But do *we* really think so?

Certain studies, notably that by Green and Levine at the University of Pennsylvania, appear to lend substance to the proposition that imports of Western technology have a great effect on the productivity of the economy, considerably greater than Soviet technology has. However, this is a highly complex and controversial matter. How does one measure the contribution of an imported machine or know-how to an increase in production to which there is also a major contribution from Soviet labor, management and equipment? How can we know how much more inefficient this process of production would have been had they chosen to develop their own technology? Every country that imports machinery presumably does so because it is more effective than any available alternative. In many cases, owing to the widespread international specialization in production of machinery, there may be no domestic alternative to the imported machine. It has been a valid criticism of the investment policies of the Soviet Union and of its Comecon allies that they have tried in the past to produce too many types of machines at home, and relied too little on international specialization. Does one measure the effect of a machine by what would happen if it were not available? In some cases it is so essential that a whole production complex is dependent upon it, at least in the short run. Another way of looking at the issues involved is to imagine that Soviet planners give systematic administrative preference to their own or to Comecon machinery, unless the Western machine is very much more effective. In a market economy one could achieve the same result by imposing a high import duty on machinery. Then, indeed, the effectiveness of imported machinery would be much higher, but I am not sure what this would prove. To avoid misunderstandings let me stress that I do *not* wish to cast doubt on the proposition that Western technology and know-how significantly benefit the Soviet Union and its allies when they import it. Of course it does! But formidable conceptual obstacles stand in the way of measuring its effect.

It is true that, while some of their imports are directly or indirectly related to the people's consumption needs (grain, wool, coffee, etc.), a much larger proportion than is economically "natural" goes to the needs of heavy industry. It is also a fact that by importing technology and know-how they expect to become more efficient and more productive, and, because they are behind the West, they can certainly learn more from us than we can from them. But in all these respects they behave as most other developing countries. The difference, as someone will doubtless point out, is that India and Venezuela do not threaten us and are not great military powers, and that anything that makes the Soviet Union more formidable is to be deplored. I will discuss this further when we come to Western policy options.

But first some other matters require attention. One is the view that by supplying them with technology and know-how we not only strengthen them (which we do), but we will enable them to relapse into autarky at a higher level: then, having acquired what they need they can be self-sufficient and trade less. The historical parallel would be the years 1928 to 1932, which were certainly followed by a very substantial reduction in Soviet purchases of machinery.

To this there are two possible replies. One is to note that the political conditions of the 1930s do not seem to be present, and that all the indications are that the Soviet Union (and even more its Comecon partners) desires to expand trade relations with the West, not to contract them (subject always to their ability to pay for imports). The second is that, in the virtually unanimous opinion of experts, the Soviet technological lag is not diminishing and will not be diminished significantly by their purchases from the West. The reason is that by the time the Soviet purchasing missions have been ordered to buy, some years will have passed from the time when the then new technology will have first been noted and considered. By the time the factory intended to house the new machines is built and is operational, they are no longer new, they are already likely to be obsolete. The latest Western techniques will be more advanced. So the process will continue.

Another argument is that we ought to charge the Soviet Union fully for research and development expenditures embodied in the equipment we sell, and also that the amount they pay is often very much below the economic effect the import has. Let me illustrate these points with examples. Thus we learn that the Soviet Union has acquired surplus American space suits at low prices, though they needed much time, effort, and money to develop. Then there is the case that Soviet long-distance transmission of electricity requires the use of imported Western switchgear, and that it would be very expensive and awkward to replace it. The moral seems to be that the price should be much higher for these reasons.

Presumably the space suits were surplus to requirements and were being sold off cheaply for the same reason as goods are disposed of through army surplus stores: there is no alternative use for them. As for the switchgear, one must recall that one does not in fact usually sell machines at a price determined by the damage the customer would suffer if the machine were suddenly denied him. So in both cases the argument is we should decide to charge the Soviet Union (and its associates too?) prices higher than normal market prices. It is hard to see how this could be administered, and few other Western countries would agree with this anyway. Naturally, sale of know-how or research results to the Soviet Union should be at a price advantageous to the seller, but no one would dispute this.

Finally, what is there in it for the West? What *is* our economic gain?

First, there is the normal gain from trade, the same as in trade with anyone else.

Second, the Eastern countries are a useful market. Some additional employment is generated in making goods to sell to them. American and Canadian farmers are not sorry when the Soviet Union buys grain.

Third, in the long run, the Soviet Union's enormous Siberian territories contain vast sources of minerals: iron ore, nonferrous metals, coal, oil, gas, as well as timber. In a world that might run short of one or several of these valuable materials, these Siberian riches could be of substantial benefit. This is not an immediate prospect, because of the remoteness of most of these riches, away in snowy wastes. But they will gradually appear, perhaps with the help of Western technology (and credits).

Fourth, it pays the West to diversify its sources of supply. It used to be said that we must not become dependent on the Soviet Union for oil, in case they used it politically, and for this reason the British (for instance) refused to allow inports of Soviet oil, until 1973 taught us all that it is not only communists who can use oil as a political weapon. (The point about the danger of *excessive* dependence is well taken.)

The relative importance of these arguments naturally varies. Thus countries with a high dependence on imported fuel and materials are attracted to projects that develop Soviet export potential; this is particularly clear in the case of Japan in relation to Siberia, as was indeed recognized in a U.S. official survey (Hardt et al., 1974), (though Japanese credits have fallen short of earlier expectations, partly due to the continuing disagreements over the Kurile islands, partly because the Japanese do not wish to offend China).

There seems no doubt that trade with the East is of *some* value economically to the West. As we have noted, as a percentage of total trade it is of greater significance to the East. Whether the transactions actually entered into benefit the East more than they benefit the West is a question which, in my view, cannot be answered; but personally I see no reason why this should be so, taking the rough with the smooth, the swings with the roundabouts. It is up to those who believe otherwise to prove their case.

Détente and Soviet External Economic Policy

It is the contention of some observers that détente had a primarily economic motivation—to get technology, grain, and credits to prop up a critically unsound economy. In my view this is so misleading as to be an invitation to policies that will fail. We do not have so much "leverage."

The errors are both economic and political. The Soviet economy's weaknesses are not critical. They are certainly serious, and while it is true that Western technology is regarded as an important way of coping with them, the system can survive without it, if necessary. This assertion can be challenged; some readers may ask: "How does he know?" I freely admit that this is a matter of judgment. In my view, assessing the often contradictory evidence, Western opinion has swung too far, from exaggerating Soviet strength (when we took too seriously Khrushchev's boasts about overtaking America) to the now fashionable total denigration. It has been 20 years since Khrushchev's boasts and the Sputnik alarmed us. Since then, the Soviet economy has grown considerably stronger and more efficient. Whether one is discussing the output of ICBMs, agriculture, housing, labor productivity, design of machinery, computers, planning techniques, or even clothing, there are qualitative and quantitative improvements. Official statistics doubtless exaggerate their extent, but very few doubt the truth of the above assertion, and these few do not include the CIA. Certainly inefficiencies remain; quality is well below world levels; planning techniques cannot cope effectively with the complexities of a modern industrial economy; the consumer is increasingly impatient with the gap between promises (and hopes) and actual progress, a gap exacerbated by economically irrational pricing and inefficient distribution, which together cause shortages, black markets, and also privileged access to scarce goods by officials of state and party. There is a growth of cynicism and corruption, and of nationalism too. There are question marks over the succession to the present septuagenarian leadership, and great irritation among the creative intelligentsia over restrictions on freedom. Far be it from me to assert or pretend that the Soviet Union is free from political and economic strains. Nor are its relations with European partners at all happy, with widespread discontent particularly prevalent in Poland and Czechoslovakia, while the Romanian party leadership takes up embarrassingly independent postures. Moscow is also showing increasing irritation at the sight of "Eurocommunism." But *we* have political and economic problems too! Comparing the Soviet Union with, say, Great Britain, Italy, Spain, or even France, which is the more unstable? The answer is not obvious.

Paradoxically, internal stability in the Soviet area is threatened by détente, since effort, order, and discipline are easier to demand and enforce if there is a visible external enemy.

Economic necessity is not, then, *the* explanation of détente, though, of course, opportunities to strengthen the economy are taken, and Western technology is imported for cash and on credit more easily in a more relaxed atmosphere.

The political error consists of seeing in détente a new policy. What new policy? What attitudes or positions has the Soviet Union abandoned, what has changed? I am *not* one of those who interpret Soviet policy in terms of the unchanging pursuit of Leninist aims of world revolution. But it has been over 20 years since Khrushchev started preaching "peaceful coexistence." In what respects is détente (a Western word anyway, not invented by the Russians) different? Khrushchev would have been happy to sign an agreement over Berlin if the West had recognized the GDR and the status quo in Europe. He would have been delighted to obtain long-term credits. These things *we* denied him. Western policy changed much more than did the Soviet attitude. We may have been wrong to change, but change we did. Surely future historians will thus interpret the often contradictory policies of the great powers in the first half of the 1970s.

It is *almost* as if we were to attribute the recent change in Chinese-American or Cuban-American relations to the conversion of Mao or Castro to the view that the United States should be recognized! Needless to say, both China and Cuba would hope to obtain some economic advantages from better relations, but that is another story.

It is fascinating to study Soviet reaction to the West's economic difficulties of recent years. On the face of it, they should rejoice. Maybe Marx's forecasts, endlessly repeated, of the "final crisis of capitalism" really will come to pass? The disarray of the West, the strains, the disorders, cannot fail to cause happiness in the hearts of Soviet diplomats. However, they seem to be of two minds; or rather, different parts of the party-state machine react differently. Those who are responsible for trade are happy to take advantage of the situation by placing orders with Western firms, thereby helping the West to reduce unemployment and lessen the impact of recession. Their propaganda stresses (overstresses, indeed) the positive effect of this on the Western economies. Some revolutionary far-left critics of Soviet policy claim that the Soviet Union is increasingly locked into the world-wide division of labor, that it has a vested interest in the stability of this conflict. The maverick Marxist André Gundar Frank (1977) devoted a whole paper to this theme, and claims to have found a truly remarkable quotation from the Bulgarian party leader, Zhivkov: "It may be hoped that the crisis that is raging in the West will come to a rapid end, since it affects and creates uncertainties for the Bulgarian economy, which to a certain extent is dependent on trade with the countries of the West."[6]

A possible parallel is the attitude of some Western statesmen, say Chancellor Schmidt and President Giscard d'Estaing. Neither is in the least sympathetic to Moscow or its aims, but evidently both prefer stability and the avoidance of risk, and to this extent are critical of President Carter's campaign for human rights, which, if successful, would be likely to have a destabilizing effect. (Perhaps the so-called Sonnenfeldt doctrine had some similar aspects to it: we would welcome the liberation of Poland, etc., from Soviet domination, but dangers to the precarious balance of power and peace are perhaps best avoided.)

The Soviet political view is doubtless also influenced by their optimistic assessment of the situation in Africa, the belief that, with a little help from them when risk is minimal, the West will be in trouble. As we know from the example of Angola, this is fully within the Soviet concept of what détente means.

But to return to the political *economy* of trade. Soviet official statements can be quoted to the effect that their trade is political. But this must be interpreted in the light of their equally official claim that their economic decisions in general are dominated by politics. So, in a sense, they are. Political men decide to expand steel production, the chemical industry, housing construction, the output of wheeled tractors or whatever. The political leadership *is* the supreme economic management of the economy. Therefore political and economic considerations are inextricably intertwined. Suppose a meeting of ministers decides, first, to increase the output of synthetic fibers; then decides that lack of the necessary equipment within the Soviet Union and Comecon makes it desirable to look to the West; and, finally, decides that the best and cheapest equipment is to be found in West Germany. Is the purchase to be regarded as meaningfully political in character? If it is, then what would be an economic decision? Of course, if in the above circumstances, it were decided to place the order in Italy instead, in order to further some political objective, politics would be directly involved.

A proportion of Soviet decisions on trade are influenced by politics, certainly. We have already mentioned a few examples. Aid programs for developing countries are another instance, though in this respect the Soviet Union does not differ from other countries. Obviously her economic relations with Comecon are greatly affected by political considerations. It is noteworthy that the economic weapon has been used most often not against capitalists but against communist heretics: three examples since the war are Yugoslavia (total boycott, 1950 to 1956), Albania (total break still), and China (withdrawal of technical aid, sharp cut in trade relations after 1959). Soviet trade deals in the 1930s with fascist Italy and Nazi Germany, and today with the Brazilian and Argentinian military regimes, are examples of the priority of economic advantage over ideological purity (though the Soviet Union does not have relations with South Africa or Israel).

Perhaps, as Lenin used to say, they hope that the capitalists will sell the rope which will be used to hang them. But, meanwhile, they tell their traders to buy the rope in the cheapest market, on economic criteria.

Then there is the not unimportant question: who are "they"? Has the Soviet Union a monolithic, unanimous approach to foreign affairs and to trade? This is a highly controversial area, but an extraordinarily interesting pamphlet by the recent emigré Alexander Yanov (1977), published recently in Berkeley, points to important elements of the ruling elite that are directly interested in enlarging contacts and interdependence (if only because they benefit materially from visits and the acquisition of consumer durables), and these same elements would suffer from tensions and cold war. There are other groups that take a more hostile stance. Which trade policies on the part of the West are more likely to strengthen which group? Yanov advocates pressure to break the ministry's monopoly on foreign trade (a monopoly already partly broken in other Eastern countries, as we have noted), but he opposes a negative attitude to trade as such, insofar as Western obstruction may have unfortunate political repercussions within the ruling elite. His analysis is a subtle one, and contains many ifs and buts. I mention it here because it does introduce another dimension into the West's policy considerations.

The "pro-interdependent" lobby in the Soviet Union does really exist. Books appear on East-West economic relations with titles such as "From Confrontation to Cooperation." Or it may be worth quoting Shmelev (1977: 80) again. He notes that

> The process of deepening of production specialization and cooperation between East and West is still in its early stage. Neither the political nor the economic (especially the investment) bases of such a process have yet seen their due development. For historical reasons there arose in both the West and East of Europe a large number of national industrial complexes with a high degree of self-sufficiency, especially in manufacturing. A negative consequence is the existence of many parallel and relatively weak national production units. However one can hardly assert that this . . . was a historic necessity. Rather has it been the consequence of artificial breaking of traditional economic ties between socialist and capitalist states.

The author blames the latter on the West. He continues: "It seems now to be realistic to discuss the possibility of some sort of coordination of long-term prospectives of development of the East and West of Europe, especially in their investment aspects."

The author advocates closer contact between Comecon and the European Common Market. His article is concerned with Europe, but the text also makes it clear that its author strongly favors closer interdependence based upon specialization and cooperation also with the United States. Appearing as it does in a Soviet journal for specialists the article is not directed to a Western audience, but seems rather to be aimed at convincing Soviet officialdom of the desirability of such a policy. Presumably, as Yanov has argued in his pamphlet, some prefer a more "isolationist" approach. Is it in our interests to prove Shmelev wrong and them right?

Political Options for the West

This finally brings us to the key questions. What is a sensible Western, or American, policy on East-West trade? What actions are desirable or feasible? What effects can we reasonably expect policy decisions in this field to have?

Let us first expound, and then analyze, the doctrines of those who consider the East-West trade, or in particular trade with the Soviet Union, as the equivalent of trading with the enemy, something undesirable, which it is our task to minimize or even to eliminate, if possible. For them the Soviet Union is a powerful military menace, hell-bent on our destruction. Anything that strengthens the Soviet Union is, by definition, bad. It is like selling scrap to Japan before Pearl Harbor. Foreign trade is one means by which the Soviet political leadership strengthens the economy. Anything that releases resources for military spending is to be deplored. But greater efficiency or productivity anywhere in the economy releases resources that could be devoted to military purposes. Conversely, given that Soviet leaders are now compelled to devote some attention to the consumer, if they were deprived of the means to greater efficiency, they would be compelled to spend more on consumer goods and agriculture, introduce serious economic reforms, reduce defense spending or become more amenable at the SALT conference table, and give a little on human rights too.

These considerations cause a number of Soviet dissidents, including Solzhenitsyn and Sakharov, to urge the West not to provide gains to the Soviet Union through trade and credits. Their views must command respect.

It should be noted that the logic of the above position is *embargo,* no trade at all. For evidently *any* gain in efficiency anywhere, whether in the production of guns or butter, Pepsi-Cola or sausages, tape decks or private cars, releases resources for other, and perhaps less agreeable, purposes. In *this* sense grain too is a strategic good, though it is eaten by Soviet citizens and animals and is therefore a consumer good. If their planners want it, it must benefit their political economy. Therefore we should only sell them goods they do not wish to buy!

However, given the political realities in Western countries, even if desirable such a policy is plainly impracticable; it was even impracticable on the morrow of so shocking an event as the invasion of Czechoslovakia in 1968.

Less drastic policy options exist, of course. Some Soviet imports can be treated as less noxious, from the above point of view, than others, and some may actually be useful in diverting resources to more desirable purposes. The obvious example is equipment to make small cars. Motorization compels all sorts of ancillary expenditures: on service stations, motels, roads, garages, etc. Also cars induce a nonideological, positively bourgeois attitude to life. So the Fiat deal could be said to be good. It is hard to see much wrong with a chewing-gum factory or Pepsi-Cola, even if they do release resources for other things. But on this view we should not, as a rule, sell modern technology. Since *modern* technology is what they wish to buy, and we do not usually produce antique technology, this means to all intents and purposes no sales of machinery and equipment. Since machinery and equipment constitute a high proportion of total Soviet purchases from the West, this means a drastic reduction in trade. In fact it means a return to the policy and atmosphere characterized by the ban on export of large-diameter oil pipe, referred to earlier when American pressure prevented the sale of an item *because* it was plainly very important for the Soviet economy at that moment to acquire it. Soviet planners would then be compelled, willy-nilly, to minimize trade dependence on the West, as an insurance against such things happening. Is this what we really want? Is it in our interests to force them into greater self-sufficiency? There is also the problem of how one administers trade under such a policy. Zbigniew Brzezinski, when he was still at Columbia University, once spoke of "calibration" as the best policy, meaning by this that each deal should be judged as to its desirability, presumably by some governmental committee. I recall the adverse reaction of American businessmen engaged in East-West trade. To have to seek permission in each instance imposes uncertainty, delay, and expense upon both the businessmen and their Soviet trade partners. Such a policy would hardly make much sense if confined to the United States, since the principal Western sellers of machinery to the Soviet Union (West Germany, Japan, France, Italy, etc.) will plainly go on selling, unless and until we reach a state of acute international crisis.

Another approach would aim to link trade deals and credits with political concessions, either in the context of SALT or on human rights. To be effective, this policy can only be based on the belief that the Soviets need our aid and trade so badly, so desperately, that they are willing to pay a political price *in addition* to the normal commercial price. Thus, some argue, if they have a drought and are short of grain, America should "use the grain weapon." If they want grain, or credits, technology, MFN, or whatever, let them accept Cyrus Vance's arms limitation proposals, order the Cubans out of Angola, let out another 50,000 Jews, and release some dissidents from camps. We have "leverage" and should use it.

On this issue, my view is pretty clear. First, as their need is not so desperate, such a policy will have no effect, except in worsening the political atmosphere. Thus a bread shortage publicly attributable to a politically motivated refusal to export grain would be positively helpful to Soviet public relations. There is also something inherently unacceptable in the proposition that if a machinery complex costs, say, $10 million, the Russians (and only they) should pay not only $10 million, but also in the form of political concessions.

This view by no means excludes behind-the-scenes horse-trading (for example, "It would help get the trade bill through Congress if you did so-and-so, or refrained from doing such-and-such"). Indeed, this sort of secret diplomacy is a good way of proceeding; secret, because it would be intolerable loss of face to be *seen* to be giving way to economic pressure. After all, larger numbers of exit visas were given for Jews than seemed possible ten years ago, and the West Germans have quietly obtained permits for ethnic Germans to return. This is a different sort of tactic to that adopted by Senator Jackson and his supporters.

Then we must consider also *what* it is that the West could demand, with any expectation of getting anything but a dusty answer. The most far-fetched idea is that we could use economic weapons to enlarge the area of freedom in the Soviet Union, or to loosen their grip on their sometimes unwilling allies. The Soviet leadership believes, and nothing in history disproves their belief, that Russia can only be ruled as an isolated autocracy. This phrase I borrow from Sir William Hayter, former British ambassador to Moscow. This view is reinforced by the opinions of many emigrés: the Soviet leaders would feel insecure; stability would be threatened; they certainly think Soviet rule *must* be accompanied by total party control (recently strongly reasserted by Brezhnev), censorship, strict limits on exchange of information and travel, with the KGB empowered to make those arrests judged necessary to prevent dangerous outbursts of nationalism or dissidence. Does this mean that the tragic legacy of Russian autocracy, translated into the language of a Communist dictatorship, will be with us forever? We all hope not. Change happens everywhere, and even the conservative-communist Muscovite regime has altered and will alter. Indeed, one can list some quite significant changes since the despot Stalin died. But change will come from internal causes, not outside pressures, which, on the contrary, can only reinforce the darkest suspicions and justify an increase in the KGB vote.

Can anyone in his right mind imagine the Soviet leadership bargaining away what they regard as essential for the security of the regime in order to obtain Western technology or grain?

The answer to this is so obvious that President Carter's insistence on raising the human rights issue plainly puzzles some Western statesmen as much as it puzzles and irritates Brezhnev. As a propaganda ploy it makes perfect sense. As a serious or a feasible policy it is very much more dubious.

Indeed, if Latin-American dictatorships, dependent on the United States for arms and markets, reject pressure to mend their dictatorial ways, what reason have we to expect anything different from the Soviet Union?

Brezhnev may not be insincere when he stresses those aspects of human rights that relate to social security, education, and the like. He recently took great pride in including in the revised constitution the citizens' right to housing. I am sure that he believes political freedom in its Western meaning is a recipe for anarchy, at least in Russia. He would perhaps agree that "political liberty is a swindle because a man doesn't spend his time being political. He spends it eating, sleeping, amusing himself a little, and working—mostly working." Or he might even agree that "We have crime in direct proportion to freedom. Lots of freedom, lots of crime." The first of these quotations is from Aldous Huxley's *Antic Hay.* The second is from an American police novel by Joseph Wambaugh. Needless to say, our Western societies give far greater freedom for the individual, and this is vitally important, not least for this author, who would surely land speedily in jail in a Soviet-ruled country. But this does not mean that the large majority of Russians care much for political freedom. Nor should we forget that even traditionally democratic Western countries are facing trouble and strife. Are our societies not a little too disordered, our own instabilities too dangerous, for us to read confident lectures to the Russians about how to organize their society, and then try to write these lectures into trade treaties? (The Russians' use of coercion to compel, say, the Czechs to organize their society the way Moscow wants it, raises rather different issues. But we will not prevent Soviet security measures in their power zone by bargaining over trade agreements.)

Foreign and military affairs could provide some more effective opportunities for action, but only if the West were much more united than is in fact the case. The Soviet Union could be informed that a repetition of Angola, or a major Soviet intervention in Ethiopia or Rhodesia, would be met by disagreeable countermeasures, including a ban on credits, for example, or cancellation of some contracts in which the Soviets are particularly interested. It may not work, but it is not impossible that it would influence the Kremlin in their consideration of whether to commit themselves to adventures that, in their eyes, could have unpleasant side-effects. No loss of face would be involved if the Politbureau at a secret meeting decided against sending modern weapons to Addis Ababa or to Mozambique.

As for strategic arms limitation, the outlook is much less promising, if my interpretation of Soviet attitudes is correct. If it is not, then of course different conclusions follow. My interpretation is that the Soviet military establishment still considers itself qualitatively behind the United States, that in all recent and actual new development (MIRV, then the cruise missile and the neutron bomb) the Americans have been and are in the lead, and that the Russians' impressive efforts are, in their eyes, a way of catching up by matching quantity against quality. Moscow's extremely negative reaction to the Cyrus Vance "package" offer seems to be based on genuine dismay: America was willing to refrain from developing her qualitative lead only on condition of a major cutback in Soviet quantity, which, as the Soviet military see it, would firmly establish American superiority and was intended so to do.

Whether or not the above hypothesis correctly describes the actual state of deployed strength and research in progress is not for a nonexpert to assert. But I imagine that even Cyrus Vance would not strongly disagree with the description above as an account of what the Russian leaders *believe* to be the position. (Remember that all military establishments, including our own, are apt to err on the side of making the worst possible assumptions concerning the capabilities of potential enemies.)

Of course, if one believes that the Soviets are *leading* in the arms race, the hope of influencing them toward moderation by economic means is not inherently absurd. But if the above view correctly represents what they believe to be the situation, then it is plainly *very* improbable that they would choose to fall behind in the arms race in order to obtain credits, machinery, and grain.

What, finally, would be a sensible Western policy toward East-West trade?

I would suggest the following principles:

1. Of course, any trade or credits *must* be advantageous to the West. We are not in the aid business.

2. Mutually advantageous deals will also profit the East. This is the nature of trade.

3. Interdependence is, on balance, good rather than bad. That is to say, a large increase in the volume of trade and long-term commitments, a greater association of Eastern economies with Western business, is a desirable objective. It is not without risk for *both* sides, in that damage could be done if a crisis caused disruption of economic links. But precisely this might strengthen mutual reluctance to push things that far. Trade is not vital enough to alter the basic course of policy; this we can take for granted. But it can make a difference when statesmen hesitate between alternatives, and, in the long run, it could soften attitudes.

4. Involved in interdependence is more human contact, more trading offices, more groups of technicians and business executives visiting the Soviet Union, more of their experts traveling West. The Soviet leaders do not like this, but that is no reason for us not to welcome it. If a French or British worker or specialist stays for six months in the Soviet Union, the likely effect is to immunize him against communisn for life. The effect of visits to the West by Soviet or Czech citizens is, shall we say, likely to have even less favorable effects from Brezhnev's point of view.

5. Some types of trade deal or credit are to be preferred from the point of view of the economic interest of particular Western countries. Thus long-term credits that develop and make available Siberian raw materials and fuels, while of course in the Soviet interest too, can be of substantial benefit to us. If payment is to be made in the material and fuel being developed (a form of "credit barter" deal that appeals to the Soviet planners), then this seems to be a sound basis for long-term business, provided the credit-terms and prices are attractive.

6. On the other hand, as already indicated, the sort of barter deal (whether on credit or not) that lays upon the Western partner the duty of selling Soviet manufactures is frequently awkward for the company concerned and not in the national interest. One must also carefully consider setting limits to the growth of Eastern debt, though a total ban on further long-term credits would be inappropriate.

7. The West could look critically at the remaining administrative barriers and discriminatory measures that impede Eastern export, in the knowledge that our own sales cannot increase (or indeed the credits already granted be repaid) unless the East can sell more. MFN treatment would do little harm and some good, if accompanied by antidumping safeguards. The chief beneficiaries from MFN would be not the Soviet Union but the smaller Comecon members, who are better able to sell manufactures in a competitive market.

8. Certain goods of direct or indirect strategic significance need to be embargoed. An appropriately revised list should be made known to all concerned, and it should then be assumed that trade in items not on the list be conducted on the Western side on normal commercial principles. Such principles include, indeed assume, hard-headed bargaining to secure the best prices and other advantages.

9. No policy can work unless the Western countries are agreed upon what it should be. America cannot go it alone because, with the exception of grain, she is not a major supplier to the East. Modern technology could simply be obtained from Western Europe and Japan. Only in a few instances is America an irreplaceable source.

The approach outlined above is controversial in America, much less so in Europe. I believe that it can be defended against all criticisms except one: the entire case falls flat on its face if Soviet foreign policy has been misinterpreted; i.e., if instead of being a great power aiming at parity and anxious to avoid dangerous confrontations, the Soviet Union is in fact preparing to challenge the West, as soon as it has the military superiority such a challenge requires. Some will even claim that it will do this in pursuit of Lenin's grand design, the master-plan forcibly to convert the world to the communist creed, *their* kind of communist creed (for the last thing they would want, on any interpretation, is a heretical communist rival such as China). I am personally convinced that the Leninist urge to world revolution has become no more than incantation for high days and holy days. But can we really be certain, beyond all reasonable doubt, that the Soviet Union (or Russian neo-Empire) will not use its military strength–if not under Brezhnev then under his unknown successors–if not for communism, then for Russian power and glory? This seems to me unlikely in the extreme, given the huge risks of nuclear war and the disarray and crisis that the Soviets must see in the West, which must surely suggest to them that it is safer and wiser to wait and see if the West disintegrates. *This* possibility should indeed cause us the gravest concern. But our disintegration, if it occurs, will be our own doing, not theirs.

So in the end the trade policy to choose must depend on one's assessment of Soviet aims and of the effect of the chosen policy on future Soviet actions. Opting for increased interdependence, based upon mutual economic advantage, seems on balance to offer more hope than the alternative.

NOTES

1. We all have "aims" which, in our circumstances, cannot be translated into action or even active intention. As one American scholar put it, if one asked Somerset Maugham, when he was 85 years old, whether he wished to sleep with Brigitte Bardot, his answer might have been yes, but for various reasons this "aim" would not have been operationally significant.

2. Nineteen seventy-five was a year when the East was heavily in debt. The figures exclude East Germany.

3. There is even a case of a Hungarian firm producing medical equipment in Great Britain with Hungarian machinery on a profit-sharing basis (Shmelev, 1977: 86).

4. Indeed, I was interpreting at the time!

5. It is well to recall that a giant U.S. corporation has a turnover greater than the total national product of one of the smaller Comecon countries!

6. I have not checked this in Bulgarian sources.

REFERENCES

Ekonomicheskie svyazi vostok-zapad (East-West Economic Relations) (1976).

FRANK, A. G. (1977) "Long live transideological enterprise." Economic and Political Weekly. Bombay (February).

HARDT, J. P. et al. (1974) Western Investments in Communist Economics. For the Committee on Foreign Relations, U.S. Senate (August 5).

SHMELEV, N. (1977) "Production and scientific-technical cooperation of the European countries." Voprosy ekonomiki 6 (June).

United Nations Economic Commission on Europe (1976a) Economic Bulletin for Europe, Vol. 28.

--- (1976b) Economic Survey of Europe, Part II.

YANOV, A. (1977) Detente after Brezhnev: The Domestic Roots of Soviet Foreign Policy. Berkeley: Institute of International Studies, University of California.